Ask Questions, Get Sales

2nd Edition

CLOSE THE DEAL
AND CREATE LONG-TERM
RELATIONSHIPS

Stephan Schiffman

Adams Media
Avon, Massachusetts

Published by Adams Media, an F+W Publications Company
57 Littlefield Street, Avon, MA 02322

ISBN: 1-59337-112-8
Printed in Canada
J I H G F E D C B

Library of Congress Cataloging-in-Publication Data
Schiffman, Stephan.
Ask questions, get sales / Stephan Schiffman.-- 2nd ed.
p.   cm.
ISBN 1-59337-112-8
1. Selling. I. Title.

HF5438.25.S3336 2004
658.85--dc22
2004013351

This publication is designed to provide accurate and authoritative information
with regard to the subject matter covered. It is sold with the understanding that
the publisher is not engaged in rendering legal, accounting, or other professional
advice. If legal advice or other expert assistance is required, the services of a
competent professional person should be sought.
  —From a *Declaration of Principles* jointly adopted by a Committee of the
American Bar Association and a Committee of Publishers and Associations

Many of the designations used by manufacturers and sellers to distinguish their
products are claimed as trademarks. Where those designations appear in this
book and Adams Media was aware of a trademark claim, the designations have
been printed with initial capital letters.

The characters and examples in this book are fictional and are used for illustra-
tion purposes only. Any resemblance to actual persons, living or dead, or actual
events or locales is entirely coincidental.

This book is available at quantity discounts for bulk purchases.
For information, please call 1-800-872-5627.

Visit our home page at *www.adamsmedia.com*

Acknowledgments

The following people helped to make this book a reality: Brandon Toropov; Lynne Einleger; Steve Bookbinder; Scott Forman; Amy Stagg; Stacia Skinner; George Richardson; Art Jackson; Alan Koval; Surendra Sewsankar; Carlos Alvarez; Martha Rios; Tina Bradshaw; Lesha Connell; David Rivera; Carlos Ortiz; Michle Reisner; and, especially, Daniele, Jennifer, and Anne, whose patience and understanding were invaluable. I'd also like to acknowledge here all the families of the salespeople of the world—the people who put up with the deadlines, the quotas, the difficult prospects, the hard sales, and all the rest of the obsessive work that's part of any good salesperson's life.

Contents

Chapter One

Getting Started

The odds are good that you bought this book with the intention of improving your questioning skills during the sales process. And that's exactly what we'll be covering here.

I'll bet you're also wondering: Who is this guy, and why should I listen to what he has to say about dealing with my prospects?

It's a fair question. Here's the answer. I run a twenty-four-year-old sales training company that has, as of this writing, trained over half a million people and has offices in New York, Toronto, Los Angeles, Chicago, Columbus, Cincinnati, Milwaukee, Philadelphia, Dallas, Houston, Boston, Long Island, Central New Jersey, and Kansas City. I started the business from scratch. We have received tremendous reviews from Amazon.com and *Selling Power* magazine; and we are number-one rated for training and prospecting. Since launching the company back in the late 1970s, I've been lucky enough to:

- Establish relationships with hundreds of the world's top companies, including Chevron-Texaco, Exxon-Mobil, Federal Express, Nextel, Chase, Waste Management, Washington Mutual Finance, Fleet Bank, and many other *Fortune* 1,000 companies
- Implement successful training programs in North America, South America, Europe, and Asia
- Write and publish twenty-three books in seven languages

When I started this business all those years ago, I didn't know it was going to be a sales training company. I thought it was going to be a consulting firm. I sat around, literally by myself, asking, "How do I create something? How do I make something happen? How do I get customers?"

To answer that question, I first printed 10,000 pens and 10,000 brochures. I decided I was going to use these to send out a mailing, but that didn't really work for me. (I still have some of the pens, if you're interested.)

What I ended up doing was learning how to make appointments. And that, fortuitously enough, was what I began building my company around: setting appointments, learning how to sell, and understanding the sales process. So what I'm going to share with you here are some things I've learned about selling—specifically, things I've learned about asking questions during face-to-face meetings with prospects.

What Is High-Efficiency Selling?

Many salespeople are taught to go in and "find pain" or "find a problem" during their meetings with prospects. Traditionally, salespeople are taught to ask about the pain, ask about the problems associated with whatever's going on in the prospect's world.

But in doing that, you actually limit yourself to a very small percentage of the situations where you could add value.

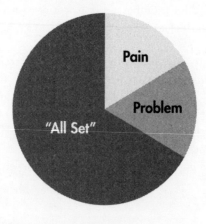

By asking about pain and problems, you basically *limit* yourself to winning sales from those people who are willing to answer "Yes" when you ask them if they have any problem or feel any pain. The rest of the people are going to be "All set." And that's what you're going to hear, over and over again. Some variation on, "We're all set."

Eventually, you'll realize what I realized after a few months of selling. *The answers we get are directly related to the questions we ask.*

We Create the Flow

In other words, you and I as salespeople create the conversational flow during all our exchanges with all the people we talk to during the course of the day.

Let's say that I sit down across from your desk and say to you, "Mister Prospect, what pain are you having right now with your current vendors?" I'm going to get an answer based on the concept of "Pain." You might say, "Yes, this is the problem; we are feeling pain about so-and-so." And I might get some degree of business from you.

There's nothing wrong with this approach when you get the business, but a large percentage of the time, you're going to say to me, "Steve, we have no problems with our vendors. *We're all set.*"

When people come to see me and try to sell to me, they often say, "Well, Mr. Schiffman, are you having any problems?" In most cases, I'm pretty happy with the vendors that I'm dealing with. So guess what I say? "Nah. *We're all set.*"

Let me give you a true story that will illustrate what I'm talking about. As a businessman, I have a longstanding personal policy about dealing with salespeople—I'll meet with just about anybody, if the person comes out and asks for the appointment. The other day a banker dropped by my office to talk to me. This particular banker has been coming to see me now for the last six years, trying to get my business. Every year, for six years, he calls up, sets an appointment, and then comes by my office and says, "Steve, are you having any problems with your bank?"

I always say, "No, things have been going pretty good for me."

And he says, "Well, you know, there's got to be something that's bothering you."

And I say, "No, not really."

I've been talking to him for six years, and he always leaves because he can't find a problem or pain. I'm always *all set* with my current bank.

Another Kind of Question

What if that banker had asked a different question altogether?

Suppose he had asked me something like this:

"Steve—just out of curiosity—how did you choose your current bank?"

If he'd asked me that question—a question based on what I had *done* in the past rather than what he thought my *pain or problem* was—then he would have gotten a very different answer, wouldn't he?

Instead of saying, "No, I don't have any problems," I would have said, "Well, I got a referral from a friend who spoke highly of the bank, and I saw that it offered a no-fee checking account, and that was interesting, so I went ahead and opened an account." (Or whatever the answer would have been.)

Now, if you agree that sales is all about encouraging a *dialogue* (and most people would not deny that it is), I have a question for you.

Which of these two approaches is *more likely* to yield a meaningful dialogue with the prospect?

1. What would you change about your current bank if you could change anything? (*Attempt to "find the pain"*)
Or:
2. How did you choose your current bank? (*Attempt to learn about what the prospect did, is doing now, or is planning to do*)

As you ponder this question, consider these two visual representations of the questioning models under discussion:

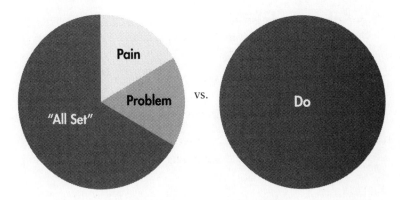

Look again at the high proportion of conversation-killing responses of "All set" that the traditional approach is likely to garner. Then consider the proportion of people (100 percent, actually) who would have something to say if you asked them a question about what they do.

Your #1 Competitor

Sometimes, during my training programs, I'll ask people, "Who's your number-one competitor?"

I'll get all kinds of answers. "The ABC Company." "The XYX Company." "Our own perceived limitations." And on and on.

Actually, those answers are not quite accurate. For most of us, the number-one competitor is *what the person you are trying to sell to is already doing.* The number-one competitor is, in fact, the status quo.

Very few of the people you are going to sit down with today, next week, next month, or next year are not already using some kind of product or service *right now.* In fact, they are all using or doing *something*—even if they are currently deciding not to use anything like what you offer.

You walk in there—and I don't care what you sell, whether you are selling banking, Internet access, training programs, paper, shipping, whatever—the fact is that every single person you are calling on *is doing something right now.* It may not be what you want them to be doing, and it may not be the way you want them to do it, but they are dong something. And it makes sense to them right now for them to do it that way.

The Sales Model

Take a look at this diagram—and consider the box that says "Close."

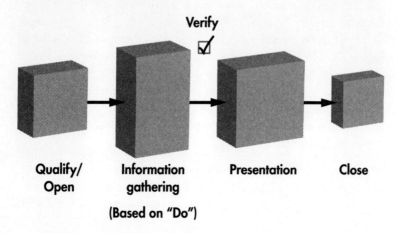

Verify ☑

Qualify/ Open   **Information gathering**   **Presentation**   **Close**

(Based on "Do")

In this sales model, you first qualify prospects as being worth your time in pursuing for a sale. Next, you gather information about them, based on asking questions related to what they "do." You make a presentation (after taking steps to verify that your presentation will meet the prospect's needs) and eventually (you hope) reach the closing stage.

But what is the "close"? What does "closing" mean?

When I ask this question, the answers I get inevitably sound like this:

"Well, we make a sale, we build a relationship, I get paid. That's what closing means."

That's certainly true. Another significant fact, however, is that the Close means that the other person actually begins to *use* your service. They bought your product and they use it. That's when the closing has definitely taken place, right? That's what makes your commission check possible.

Close = Use!

Let me give you an example of what I mean. Think of the nationally recognized courier companies like Airborne Express, Federal Express, Air Express International, and DHL. At these companies the fact that you open an account with them means absolutely nothing . . . *if you don't actually use the service.* There are plenty of accounts at those companies that are underused or aren't being used at all! Clearly, their "customer base" is the people who actually use the service. Ultimately, it's the same for you and me.

So what are we doing as salespeople? We're trying to get people to *use* the service that we offer—*forever.*

That's what the sale is, and that is *all* the sale is: The other person's decision to use the service forever. That's what we get paid for.

Now if that's true—and obviously I think it is—then what are the implications of this (deceptively) simple-sounding principle? Take a look back at the sales model.

Why is the person going to decide to use what you offer? On some level, I think you already know the answer to that question. Because it *makes sense* for him or her to do so.

In other words, if you are going back for a meeting, your aim has to be to get to the point where the person will say to themselves, *"You know what? This concept, this sale, this presentation makes sense to me."*

In other words, when it makes sense for the other person to use your product or service—that's the close. That's what it all comes down to.

Look at it this way: Whatever it is that you are doing right now professionally—it *made sense* for you at one point in your life to undertake that job, that mission, that role. That's why you decided to do what you're doing now, right? It made sense to you, based on your options at the time. It's the same with your prospects. They do what makes sense to them, based on their options at the time.

So, what's the presentation? Look at the second box over from the right in the sales model. This box represents you *presenting a plan* or *giving a reason* for someone to buy or to use your service. If that reason makes sense, the person will buy from you. If that reason does not make sense, the person will not buy from you.

In order to make a recommendation that *makes sense,* we've got to get information. Take one more look at the sales model diagram. Notice how big that information-gathering box is when compared to all the others!

If we do our job right, 75 percent of the work we do as salespeople is completed *before* we make a presentation. You'll notice that there is a verifying substep between the information step and the presentation step. That's where we confirm that what we're about to recommend is correct. To do this, I suggest you use a "preliminary proposal" or "outline proposal" before delivering a formal recommendation. (See Appendices B and C.)

The point to remember is that getting the information is absolutely crucial to success in sales—and that it's the exact opposite of "pain-based" or "problem-based" selling.

If you go in for a first meeting with someone and simply say to the person, "What pain, what problem are you having? What would you change about what you're doing right now?"—nine times out of ten you're not going to get any meaningful information. Most of the time, what you recommend *will not make sense.*

Suppose, though, you were to build your meeting around questions like this:

1. What do you do?
2. How do you do it?
3. When and where do you do it?
4. Why do you do it that way?
5. Who are you doing it with?
6. How can we help you do it better?

If you ask questions like these, you will get better, more descriptive answers from your prospects, and you'll be in a better position to establish a dialogue.

Learning how to ask intelligent variations on these six questions is what this book is all about. By the time you're done with the book, you're actually going to be able to get better information during your meetings and phone conversations because you'll be establishing a better platform from which to sell. You'll be looking at a bigger picture because you'll be asking questions in six specific areas:

Question Group #1: What the prospect does.

Question Group #2: How the prospect does that.

Question Group #3: When and where the prospect does what he or she does.

Question Group #4: Why the prospect does it that way.

Question Group #5: Who the prospect is currently working with.

Question Group #6: (Advanced—only ask after you've addressed numbers one through five.) Whether and how you can help the client do what he or she does better.

When you make a conscious choice to ask questions in these six areas, you'll find that you get much more substantial answers—and that you're gathering the information you need to make a more substantial presentation. In other words, you'll be compiling the data needed to develop a presentation that is likely to *make sense* to the other person.

Let me give you an example of what I mean—and how this "do-based" model can improve your results. At my company, we sell sales training. So the first question I ask prospects is, "What kind of sales training do you do?" I get a very different answer to that question than I would if I said, "I'm just curious, what pain or problem are you having right now?" It gives me a deeper sale and allows me to gather information that may not be based in any pain or problem the other person is experiencing.

In my selling cycle, I ask these kinds of "do" questions during the first appointment, and then I schedule a second appointment, and perhaps a third. At that point, I've not only gathered but verified my information (you remember the verification substep from our diagram), and I'm in a great position to say something like the following: "You know what? Based on what you are saying, and based upon all the information you've given me, I really think I can help you." And that results in sales.

Selling is nothing more—and nothing less—than finding out what people do and then finding ways to help them do it better.

Once we understand that, we realize that success in selling to people revolves around *finding out what they do*. If we understand what they do and how to apply that knowledge to our business, and if we understand what I call *product malleability*, we're going to sell more effectively.

Product Malleability

It's important to understand what the prospect does; it's also important, of course, to understand what *we* do.

I understand my product; more importantly, I understand how I can adapt my product to help you do what you are doing better. That's where *product malleability* comes in.

Malleability means "the ability to be shaped into another form." For me, product malleability means being able to address problems that people wouldn't normally associate with a sales training company. I have lots of success stories ready to tell, at the drop of a hat, stories that illustrate how what my company offers has been applied *creatively* to different situations—situations that my prospect might not have thought about yet.

If I understand exactly what the other person *does*, and I also understand how to adapt or shape exactly what I *offer*, then moving through the sales cycle is going to be a lot easier for me.

You Create the Flow

You create the flow of the sales conversation.

You really do. You could walk in on a sales call and say, "Hey, how are you doing today, I'd love to have a Coca-Cola." The other person will respond in kind.

Or you could walk in and say, "Hey, it's raining today." And the other person will respond in kind to that.

You could walk in and say, "You know, Mr. Jones, you're a real jerk." And Mr. Jones would respond in kind to that by showing you the way out.

The fact is that no matter what you say, people will respond to you *based on the issues you've raised yourself.*

So it behooves us as salespeople to think strategically about all the issues we raise when we ask a question. Are they really the issues we want to raise?

Hundreds of thousands of salespeople start their prospecting calls by asking the other person, whom they have never met, "How are you today?" Is that the best way to begin the conversation?

When you ask intelligent questions, you are really asking two sets of questions.

1. You're asking the person *individually* what they do, how they do it, when they do it, and why they do it that way, and then (and only then) you are going to ask questions that help you help them do it better.

2. You are also asking about the *company* because you want to know why the company is doing it, how the company got there, and what it is the company is trying to do and accomplish.

Let's say I'm selling carpeting, and I walk into a hotel. I look at the carpeting in the hotel and I say, "My God, they have beautiful carpeting." I want to sell carpeting, so what I'm going to do is try to find the right person. I'll go to who I think the right person is and I'll say, "Mr. Jones, I noticed the beautiful blue carpeting you have out there. I'm curious, how did you end up picking that, why did you buy that carpeting, how did you end up making that decision, who did you buy it from?"

That's "do-based" questioning. It's not the way people usually sell.

Case in point: A salesperson came into my office recently. He wanted to update my computers. He sat down and asked me, "Mr. Schiffman, are your computers fast enough?"

Guess what? I don't know how to answer that question. So I pointed toward my monitor and said, "You tell me. It looks fast to me." He was mortally embarrassed. He got up and left. There was nothing else to do.

A better question might have been, "Hey, I'm just curious, how did you end up with the computers you are using? How did you get the system installed? Why did you choose this system?" Even if I didn't know the answers to those questions, I would have been inclined to point him toward the person in my organization who does.

A True Story

A young salesperson comes into my office to see me; he happens to be selling Yellow Pages. He walks into the office and sits outside in the waiting area for me. I know that the meeting is going to take place, but I have to go outside for a minute. Immediately he grabs my arm and says, "Mr. Schiffman, I can help you."

I tell him we can discuss that in a minute, but before I leave, I turn to him and say, "Listen, before we begin, I'm curious—how long have you been selling Yellow Pages?" He says six years. I say, "All right, what's your number-one question? What's the first thing you're going to ask me?"

He says, "Well, Steve, I usually say to the prospect, 'Are you happy with your advertising?'"

I ask him how people respond to that.

He says, "Most people are pretty happy with their advertising."

I say, "What happens after that?"

He thinks for a moment, and then he says, "Well, I usually leave."

I say, "Do me a favor and open up that copy of the Yellow Pages. See if you can find my name or my company."

He turns the pages and turns the pages, and he can't find it. I'm not in the Yellow Pages. He looks up at me and says, "You know what, you're not in the Yellow Pages."

I say, "Bingo. So what should your first question be?"

He has no idea what I'm talking about.

Do you?

His first question should be:

"I'm just curious, Mr. Schiffman, how come you're not in the Yellow Pages?"

That's a "do-based" question!

So I tell him to ask me that question. I say, "When you see me again in two minutes, I want you to ask me why I'm not in the Yellow Pages. Then maybe we can have a real conversation."

A couple of minutes later, I go back into my office, and the Yellow Pages guy comes in. He says, "Can I ask you one question?"

I say, "Sure."

He says, "Are you happy with your advertising?"

Another True Story

I go into a California mall a number of months ago, and I go to Brooks Brothers because I want to buy a pair of suspenders. That is exactly what I have in mind: a pair of suspenders. Nothing more.

So there I am. It's a Saturday morning about nine o'clock, just when the store is opening. I walk into Brooks Brothers, see the guy at the counter, and I say, "Suspenders." (I'm a New Yorker—we don't have long conversations.)

The man at the counter responds in kind by saying, "Over there." I go over there; I'm there because that's where he said to go. He didn't ask me anything else; he just said, "Over there." I go over there, take down the suspenders, look at them, choose one, and come back. He asks me, "How are you going to pay?" I give him a card, and then I walk out.

That was the extent of the conversation. There was nothing else that went on; *but I did walk into that store.* Please remember that I did do that.

Then I go around the corner to Circuit City to buy a $20 clock radio. I know what I want; I have it in mind: a $20 clock radio. That's all I want. The young rep, the greeter, is standing by the door; and as I walk in, she says to me, "Welcome to Circuit City."

I say, "Right. Clock radios." (Again—I'm a New Yorker.)

"Oh, clock radios," she says. "That's great. We've got a big selection." And she takes two or three steps to show me where they are. Then, without missing a beat, she turns to me and says, "Can I ask you a question?"

I say, "Sure."

She says, "Just out of curiosity, what brought you into the store?"

I say, "Well, I want to buy a clock radio."

She says, "But why did you decide to buy a clock radio *today?*"

"Well," I tell her, "I just bought a house out here, and I don't have a clock radio."

"That's interesting," she says. "By the way, do you have a television?"

I realize I *don't* have a television. I let her show me the televisions.

"By the way," she says, "do you have a stereo?"

I realize I *don't* have a stereo. I let her show me the stereos.

She asks some more questions. She shows me some more stuff.

Two thousand dollars later, I walk out of the store with my clock radio.

And some other stuff.

Getting to the Deeper Sale

Look at the difference between the two salespeople above. The electronics store person created the flow of the conversation—she built the conversation around understanding *why* I walked into the store that day. The menswear store person never created a conversation to ask why I came into the store. So he got less of a sale. It isn't that he didn't get a sale; it's that he got less of a sale. She got the deeper sale because she asked me one important question based on what I was actually *doing*.

Let's say you're working with existing accounts, and you get a telephone call. The account calls you up and says, "Mr. Jones, I'm looking for that particular item in green." Your aim should not be to simply fulfill that order. Your job is to sell, and your question to him should be, "Why green?"

When I meet with prospects that have called us and asked to meet with me personally, I ask, "I'm just curious. I know you want to do sales training, but how did you reach that conclusion?" The person sitting across the desk from me will usually say something like, "We want to increase sales." I'll say, "No, I'm sure that's true, you want to do sales training because you want to increase sales, but how did you reach that conclusion? How did you decide that sales training was the right way to do that?"

Now, that sounds like I'm going to kill my sale, doesn't it?

Actually, I get *great* information as a result of that question! Typically, I find out whether my prospect is talking to any of my competitors . . . who those competitors are . . . and why the contact decided to get in touch with those competitors. Please understand what I'm telling you here: When I ask prospects this question, they often *volunteer* information about which other companies they're talking to about training and *why* they're talking to those people.

Wouldn't you rather have that information about competitors than not have it?

Let me give you another example. Lucy, a decision maker at a major life insurance company, decides they are going to change travel agencies. They have a five- or six-million-dollar travel budget and they decide they are going to change from one travel agency to another. So, Lucy puts out bids and five or six companies respond to the bid. They then come in and all of them make tremendous presentations. What are her criteria for selecting a vendor, do you think?

When I ask that question, people in my seminars say things like price. Or service. Or the fact that someone else in the company prefers another agency.

Actually, *none* of those things are what drives Lucy's decision. She picks the new vendor based on one overriding factor: *Where they are located*. She's tired of making calls to the agency in the morning and not being able to reach them because of the time zone difference. And *not one vendor* bothered to ask why she had decided to switch travel agencies!

So Lucy's evaluating your agency according to one criteria— where you're located and whether you're going to be able to answer her call in the morning. Wouldn't you rather have information like that *before* you spend a lot of time and energy developing a proposal for this person?

If the answer is "yes"—you should *ask do-based questions*. Learning how to do that effectively is what this book is all about.

Chapter Two

The Most Important Question You Can Ask

I was interviewed a couple of months ago on a radio program. The interviewer said, "Steve, what's the single most important question in sales?"

I said, "The most important question in sales is 'Why?' And you can couple that with the word 'how.'"

For example:

- *Why* are you trying to find another travel agency?
- *How* are you going to choose who you'll be working with?
- *Why* did you decide to call us today?
- *How* are you going to use the widgets you're looking for?

Once I understand *why* and *how*, I can gather the right information about what this person is actually doing. If I do that, I'm going to be more successful.

Unfortunately, instead of asking any substantive questions at all, some salespeople meet with prospects all the time and look for an excuse to pull out their brochure and read it out loud.

What a joke!

How do you feel when that happens to you? What's your reaction when the salesperson pulls out the brochure and says, "Let me tell you about . . ."

Don't your eyes start to glaze over?

If salespeople ask any questions, they usually ask questions about the product or service the prospect is using, or they start to talk about the benefits. "Let me tell you about how we can save you money . . ." Or: "Let me tell you about how we can save you time . . ." Or: "Let me tell you about how we can improve your efficiency . . ."

Often, that's the first thing they say! In other words—they may not ask anything at all!

Here are some better ways to start the meeting:

"Have you ever worked with another company like ours before?"
Or:
"Have you ever met with anyone from my company before?" (Wouldn't you want to know?)
Or:
"Have you ever thought about working with us in the past?" (Again: Wouldn't you want to know?)

Asking *any* of these questions will, I guarantee, uncover much more meaningful information than starting the business relationship by saying, "Let me tell you about . . ."

Examples to Follow—and to Avoid

I have two more stories I'd like to share with you.

Throughout this book, we'll be discussing how proper questioning during the sales process can increase your efficiency, your commission checks, and your satisfaction on the job. As we do so, we'll be returning to the following two stories from time to time. They represent the two extremes of how to ask—and how not to ask—questions when you're interacting with your prospects and customers. One of the stories, the first one, is a happy one; the other is a sad one. The happy one is, alas, much less common than the sad one . . . for most sales reps, at any rate. But don't worry. For the sales rep who manages to excel, to stand out from the crowd, and to take control of his career—for *you*, in other words—the happy story is much more typical.

Both of the stories are true; both took place during real-life sales visits. I've heard hundreds of sales-related stories over the years in my capacity as a sales trainer. When it comes to illustrating the best and worst possible outcomes that can result from different questioning techniques, I think these two anecdotes pretty much cover the spectrum.

Mark's Presentation

Three high officials at a major international telecommunications corporation had set aside a single day for presentations from the representatives of four different training firms. At stake: a lucrative multiday training seminar at a preset scheduled company gathering.

One sales rep, Mark, represented the smallest of these four firms. He knew the target company was not in the habit of going cut-rate, and he knew there was a lot of money on the line if he could win the three officials over during his presentation. As he settled into his flight to the company's headquarters in Arizona, he had a sinking feeling that he was going to find himself going up against the best and most expensive presentations his competition had to offer. This made him a little uneasy, because the seminar company he was working for was competing under a very limited budget, and he didn't have much in the way of flash or technical glitz to supplement his message. As a matter of fact, he hadn't brought anything that couldn't fit in his briefcase.

The morning the meetings were scheduled, Mark found to his dismay that he was to give his presentation fourth and that no fixed time slot had been set aside for him. This meant that he had to sit for hours in the lobby of the target company's headquarters with his briefcase perched on his lap, exchanging polite nods with his competitors. They were all carrying lots of equipment, and they all seemed extremely confident.

Mark spent a lot of time waiting that day; at one point he happened to overhear a call one of the competing reps placed on their cell phone. Mark learned that one of his company's rivals had flown in not only the sales rep to explain the seminar, but the actual trainer who would conduct it once the contract was awarded! Talk about cocky. Mark had to admit that he himself would have been just a little impressed with such a maneuver if he had been on the receiving end. The bring-the-trainer-along gambit was just the sort of high-octane, supercharged approach he'd been afraid he'd be up against. Now he knew he was right.

After forty-five minutes, the first competitor finished his presentation. Then, after another hour, the second competitor emerged from the room. After a half-hour lunch break, Mark returned to his assigned seat and watched as his third competitor—the one who had brought the real, live trainer along with him—guided his charts, his slides, his handouts, and his companion into the room.

The third competitor took more than an hour and a half to make his pitch.

Toward the end of that time, Mark began to wonder how on earth he was going to be able to keep up with the three companies that had preceded him. When his name was finally called, Mark had resolved on exactly what he would have to do if he wanted to stand any chance of pulling this sale out of the fire.

Mark made his way to the conference room with only his briefcase in his hand. There he saw three bleary-eyed, exhausted senior executives sitting dispiritedly around a small table. Before he sat down, he surveyed the room. The accumulated debris of three, high-powered, full-colored, 3-D, state-of-the-art presentations was scattered everywhere. Charts were on the wall; color foldout books were stacked on the floor; a slide projector shone a blank light on a bare screen. Mark looked again to the table where the three executives, who had clearly seen all the glitz they could handle for one day, were nevertheless waiting for him to begin the final onslaught on their senses. The men did not look happy.

Mark sat down. One of the executives, the vice president of finance, asked him if he'd need the slide projector moved closer. No, Mark replied, there would be no slides.

The three executives seemed to sit up a little straighter. One of them actually seemed to manage a smile.

"Before I get started," Mark said, "can I just ask you all one question?"

"Sure," the vice president of finance answered.

Mark smiled, looked around, and then returned his gaze to the three men at the table.

"What exactly," he asked, "is your company trying to accomplish with this program you have scheduled?"

There was a stunned silence. The three men exchanged glances with one another, and the vice president of finance looked Mark right in the eye and smiled.

"Do you know, Mark," he said, "that you are the only person who has asked us that all day?"

The other two executives laughed softly. Mark nodded and then retrieved a yellow note pad and a pen from his briefcase. Using only this low-tech equipment, he took detailed notes as the vice president of finance, who was apparently tired of being talked at all day long, delivered a thirty-minute outline of exactly what had motivated senior management to schedule the company gathering in the first place. Mark learned that the seminars were not simply intended to help the company's sales force achieve better results. (He found out later that improving sales levels was the only thing all three of his competitors had focused on during their presentations.) The vice president then explained that the seminars were also intended to help alter the corporate culture of the organization as a whole and to impart a new customer-focused message that would, in due course, be communicated to every single employee in the company. In addition, Mark learned that the company's senior managers were hoping to use the seminars as a means of developing a number of important new managers they'd brought on board.

At the end of the vice president's account of what he and the other senior managers were after, Mark offered a short summary of his own company's history and briefly laid out its history in developing long-term training projects. After five minutes of introduction to his firm, Mark summarized what he saw as his company's strongest points over its competitors, and then said this:

"You've given me a lot to think about today—may I come back next week with some ideas on how we can help you do this? I'd like to get some more of your input before we develop a formal proposal."

The three men at the table nodded. Then the vice president of finance said, "That's an excellent idea, Mark. And I think when you come, that we should make sure you get a chance to talk to the president of our company, so you can outline your recommendations for him face-to-face. Let's get his assistant on the line for you, and we can set up the time right now." Mark set up the appointment, shook hands, smiled, and left.

At the conclusion of his meeting the following week with the same three senior executives and the president of the company, he won commitments not only for the original seminar he had shown up to pitch for, but five additional programs dealing with other areas of the company as well!

Alice's Sales Call

Our next story is a much sadder one. My office needed a new telephone system, so we scheduled a meeting with the young woman who represented a company that handled business phone systems. She happened to call us one busy Friday afternoon while we were in our "search" mode—that is to say, we were evaluating the pros and cons of a number of phone systems people were proposing to us.

The meeting was scheduled for 8:00 A.M. sharp one Monday morning, and this young woman, whom I'll call Alice, was right on time. She stepped into my work area confidently, looked me straight in the eye, extended a perspiration-free hand, said my name clearly and correctly, and told me she was very glad to meet me. She looked professional, poised, and informed. She looked, in short, like a person who had all of the answers. From my perspective as a sales trainer, I can tell you that she also looked like someone who had carefully observed every rule offered in the "win-sales-by-making-a-great-first-impression" sweepstakes. I'm not suggesting that anything in her initial presentation and greeting was faulty, mind you, but read on.

At this point, I have to let you in on something about the way my office was laid out at the time I met with Alice. I used the space not only to conduct my own business correspondence, handle my own scheduling, and make phone calls, but also, from time to time, to monitor the sales calls my people made with prospects during the course of the day. I did this by means of a second phone line that led directly to my desk, a line that could be connected to the adjoining suite where my sales reps worked. I could patch in on any line they used at any given moment. (I should also mention that at my company, as at many others, all the prospects whose conversations are monitored in this way are informed at the outset of the call that the discussion with my employees may be monitored for training purposes.)

At the time I met with Alice, I had that second phone on the upper central portion of my desk, directly across from the chair occupied by visitors who came to meet with me.

Once Alice settled into her seat, she exchanged a few standard pleasantries with me. She offered complimentary assessments of the knickknacks that are situated around my desk; she admired the view.

Alice then asked me, "How's business these days, Mr. Schiffman?"

"Good," I replied. "We just wrapped up a major training program with Garden Grove Health Care, a six-day affair, a real landmark event for us."

"Is that right? Gee, that's great," she responded, smiling graciously. Then, without pursuing this potentially critical piece of prospect information a single millimeter further, she started doing what she had come to do. Alice started talking at me.

"Mr. Schiffman," she said, "let me tell you a little bit about what our company can do for you. We've got a unit called the Expanding Outlet Scale System that is designed specifically for businesses your size. I think it's probably right within your price range, though we can talk about that later. Now the Expanding Outlet Scale System has a number of important benefits for a business like yours, and I want to show you some materials that will clarify exactly what those benefits are . . ."

And with that, Alice was off to the races. She had a four-color brochure about the Expanding Outlet Scale System that she was kind enough to unfold for me on my desk. (She had to move my special training/monitoring phone out of the way to do so, but that didn't take too long.) After she'd unfolded the brochure and set it at a cock-eyed angle so I could almost make sense of what was written on it, Alice was obliging enough to read me the contents of that brochure, word for word, as I sat patiently and listened, nodding whenever she glanced up at me purposefully. My guess is that she engaged in this glancing game because she'd been taught that periodically staring the prospect down in this way is supposed to "build rapport." It could have been any of a number of sales-training programs out there that insisted to Alice that she must attend to me in this "look deep into my eyes" fashion. Alice's use of this technique seemed to assume that the mere fact of making eye contact with me was supposed to launch me into some hypnotic state that would induce me to immediately sign an agreement—once she moved from reciting the contents of her brochure at me to reciting the contents of her contract.

Alas, Alice and I never got that far. When she finished reading her speech from the brochure, I informed her that the Expanding Outlet Scale System didn't look to me as if it would meet our needs. Did Alice ask me to elaborate on this? No.

Instead, she started reciting "success stories" from other customers (clearly a preprogrammed response to the "initial objection" I had raised). I told her that the companies she mentioned all seemed a good deal larger than my firm was at that time—that they had hundreds of phone lines to deal with, and that my own staff was more in the twenty- to forty-line range.

Having been offered, through my initiative, this specific, critical piece of prospect-related intelligence, did Alice pursue it? No.

She made one last, forlorn try to convince me that the Expanding Outlet Scale System was exactly right for my business. I restated my firm conviction that it wasn't. She thanked me for my time, stood up, handed me her card, told me to call her if I ever decided to change my mind—with the pleasant, unspoken implication that I should call her if I ever saw the light and realized that the system was in fact right for my company—and shook my hand. Then she walked out.

Now I want to be very clear on one point: Alice was not rude or overbearing or dismissive toward me at any time during our meeting. She was pleasant, she was persistent, and she was polite at all times. She was certainly engaging enough to convince me that she was out to do the very best job she could for me. She was, in short, determined to leave that good first impression that someone had obviously told her was of critical importance in building business relationships. But as she left my office, it wasn't her professional attire, her crisp delivery, or her snazzy sales brochures that had formed that first impression for the prospect she had just lost. I formed my first impression based on the following observation:

During the entire fifteen-minute meeting, Alice had not once asked me why I had two phones on my desk.

Even though that second telephone was literally right under her nose as we began our meeting, and even though Alice was trying to sell me a telephone system, my other phone simply didn't exist for Alice. She was too concerned about all the other stuff that was on the checklist that someone had drummed into her head. Shake hands confidently. Look the prospect in the eye. Show off the snazzy brochure. Read it word for word. When the prospect expresses an objection, respond by highlighting the "need" you've identified and eliminated for other customers. Convince the prospect you can fill that need for him as well.

The Product Dump

At my company, we have a name for what Alice did to me during that brief meeting. We call it executing a *product dump*.

Now, I won't lie to you. In some cases, dumping on the prospect will be followed by a sale. And I think that simple fact is the reason so many, many sales trainers haven't taken the trouble to tell people not to dump on the prospect. But I'm here to tell you that real sales success—by which I mean real, serious, continuing commission revenue—is totally incompatible with this approach.

If you want to excel in your sales work, you have to abandon forever the idea of shoehorning the prospect into a preassigned slot that seems to work pretty well for some of your other accounts. You have to abandon Alice's approach for trying to convince the prospect. And, having forever abandoned that technique, you have to train yourself to ask the right questions and listen to what you hear in response.

This is not easy to do. I've worked with salespeople all over the world, in virtually every industry you can name, and I've seen firsthand how many of them incorporate Alice's approach, typically after spending some years working that way. The truth is, most of us have been deceived—and often by some very authoritative-sounding people—into believing that dumping on the prospect works. The sad truth is that it simply doesn't. It just happens to be followed, at times, by orders. And those orders are approved, not by new long-term partners, which is what you have to develop in today's often ruthless business environment, but by people who probably would have bought from you anyway—and who won't hesitate to buy from someone else the next time a deal that looks better comes along!

Asking about the Cow

Suppose you were to walk into a prospect's office, and suppose you noticed a large brown cow in front of the person's desk, munching away at a pile of hay.

What would you do?

I know what *I'd* do. I'd say hello to the person and then I'd ask, "I was just wondering: Why have you got a cow in the office?"

That makes sense, doesn't it? I'd be asking about the obvious. I'd be asking about something that's absolutely impossible to ignore.

Here's the point: How many salespeople ask the obvious questions about the obvious things, the things you couldn't possibly ignore?

For instance: You know the person you're meeting with for the first time *isn't* a customer of yours. In fact, that's just about *all* you know of any consequence.

So why not ask a question about the obvious? Why not ask a question about the cow that's in the middle of the office?

In other words—why not ask a question like this:

"I checked my records, and I noticed you're not on our customer list. I'm just curious—why not?" (Why wouldn't you want to know that?)

I had somebody come into my office to try to sell me a mobile phone. I didn't buy from him, but I did suggest that he use this question to open his next meeting with a prospect.

Later, he called me back and told me that, by opening the meeting with this question, he was able to launch a great conversation with the prospect . . . and eventually sold fifty-five cell phones to that contact!

Know When to Walk Away

Suppose Alice had taken the time to follow up the various leads I had offered her? Suppose she had learned, as an indisputable fact, that none of the systems her company handled have the slightest application to my business? And suppose further that I didn't know that? What should Alice have done?

That seemingly arcane question brings us to the only catch you'll find in this book. This book takes as a given the notion that, if your questioning indicates that the possibility for a good fit between your company and a prospect doesn't exist, you will walk away from the sale rather than try to implement something that is unlikely to help the prospect. This notion tends to thoroughly befuddle all the Alices of the world—"What do you mean, I have to say no to an order?"—but it's an idea the Marks out there use to their professional advantage. By honestly assessing their situation and the prospect's, and by making it clear from the outset that this is what we're doing, the Marks out there build long-term alliances, not short-term sales.

During my training seminars, I make no apologies for placing a good deal of the emphasis on this walk-away-from-the-sale issue. I tell people, in no uncertain terms, that they are professionals, and, as such, their commitment is to implement not just any solution, but the right solution for their customers—even if this commitment costs them a purchase order right now. This is the principle I've used to guide my own sales throughout my career, and it is one that you should use, too.

My bet is that you've probably already accepted this idea on some intuitive level. As a professional, you probably already know that, in the long run, it's better to lose a sale than to lose sleep. You must never give up your own integrity, and you must never trade a long-term business ally for a short-term sale.

Listening vs. Talking

Mark's story and Alice's story represent two very different ways of asking questions during your sales work. Mark's is incisive, inclusive, nonthreatening, and geared toward gathering information. Alice's is ritualistic, exclusive, potentially threatening (when executed by someone less polite than Alice, which is an all-too-common occurrence) and geared toward getting the prospect to be quiet so you can talk about whatever it is you've shown up to talk about.

I know there are lots of sales trainers who will tell you that I haven't done Alice justice here. They'll tell you that, because she was unfailingly polite, she can't be accused of trying to steamroll the prospect. They'll tell you that Alice used her questions to "open up the prospect," or "create a positive environment for the presentation," or "build rapport." Those sales trainers are wrong.

When you come right down to it, Mark came to listen. Alice came to talk. And a truckload of buzzwords and flashy explanations about interpersonal communication patterns can't change that.

Ready for a late-breaking news flash? Prospects like to be listened to more than they like to be talked at.

And yet, as I observed earlier, the approach Alice took during her initial contact with the prospect is far, far more common than Mark's. That's a fact of sales life, and it's nothing to be afraid of. I'm willing to bet that, if you stop right now and take stock of your own experiences with salespeople, you'll be able to come up with far more exchanges that seemed to follow Alice's pattern than exchanges that remind you of Mark's.

If, in your own work, you realize that you really can't call to mind even one exchange with the prospect that reminds you of Mark's discussion about seminar objectives with the three senior executives— don't beat yourself up. Virtually every salesperson, myself very much included, goes through a phase in which he or she sees prospects as objects of one kind or another, numbers on the page to be manipulated or "closed" or otherwise enticed into seeing whatever solution our organization can offer them. Most of us start out thinking that way. It's not because we're bad salespeople. Far from it!

Usually, we know in our hearts, or think we know in our hearts, that what we have to offer really can work for the prospect. Most salespeople (the responsible ones, at any rate) approach their work having made the assumption that something we can do can fix the problems of our potential customers.

That's not a bad mindset. That's a great mindset. It's essential to anything resembling a successful, satisfying career as a salesperson.

But it's not enough.

The Next Level

To do the best we're capable of doing, not only for ourselves, but also for our customers—we have to move up to the next level. That doesn't mean we give up the idea that we know what it takes to satisfy our customers. And it certainly doesn't mean that we forget about the strategic advantage of collecting anecdotal evidence that details the successes we've been able to bring to customers in the past. But to perform at the optimum sales level—a level that keeps the most customers coming back to us and leads to the hefty commission checks—we have to accept the notion that the prospect knows more about his or her situation than we do.

Now that doesn't seem a particularly radical notion on the surface, does it? In fact, I'd be willing to wager a thousand dollars that if you and I sat down and canvassed 500 salespeople, asking them whether they agree with the idea that the prospect typically possesses more essential information about the target organization that the salesperson does not, the vast majority of those 500 salespeople, if not every single one of them, would answer in the affirmative.

That resounding majority, however, would not change the fact that our first natural instinct, when it comes to dealing with prospects, is to show prospects what we can do for them—because that's what we know about! Having worked with as many salespeople as I have over the years, I can vouch that the let-me-show-you-what-we-can-do-for-you instinct is initially, at least, usually more than strong enough to completely overpower any instinct to find out what challenges the prospect faces in his organization. In fact, I believe that most salespeople, given the choice, would prefer not to know the specifics of how (or whether) their product or service is working once they've closed a sale. Why don't we want to know? Because we want to believe that what we have to offer works, and we often lack the technical knowledge to resolve (or even to understand) the problems that follow after the sale is "closed."

Do the ideas I'm outlining hit a nerve when you consider them in light of your own sales performance? Do they remind you of specific instances in which you lost the sale to a competitor who somehow managed to implement a glove-fitting solution to a problem one of your prospects faced—a problem you had no idea even existed? Can you think of presentations in which your product or service somehow failed to resonate at all with the prospect who "should" have had the same "need" that you had previously identified, and resolved, for prospects who seemed to you very similar to the person you were talking to?

Now here comes the really tough question. It's a question that people who've managed to carve a successful, fulfilling, and consistently lucrative career out of their sales work usually can answer with a "yes." By the same token, people who feel frustrated in their sales work, who miss quotas, whose stress levels are too high, and who can't seem to build repeat business no matter what they do—these people usually answer "no."

Can you remember the last time that, at some point during the early stages of your relationship with a contact, you asked that person, in some way, to tell you what his or her principal goal was?

Before you answer, let me clarify something. I'm not talking about times you asked the prospect to confirm some objective you *assumed* he or she wanted to get accomplished or to comment on some objective that directly related to something you considered a benefit of your product or service. I'm not interested in whether you asked the prospect technical questions about the specific elements of the widget (or widget service) you were trying to win an order for. I'm not interested in whether you asked the question that was designed to highlight an advantage you felt you offered over a competitor. I'm not interested, in other words, in questions you asked to which you knew the answer.

What I'm interested in is the last time you began your relationship with the prospect by making an effort to find out exactly what his or her key business aim was, regardless of how that aim was related to what you had to offer.

If you're like most of us, you probably had some trouble coming up with an example. If you could honestly recall such an instance, congratulations—this book will show you how to hasten your progress along this path, and it will outline specific ways you can ask questions even more effectively than you do now.

I raise these issues not to make trouble, assign blame, or make you feel bad about your work, but simply as a fellow salesperson who knows that realizing where we are is the first part of getting to where we want to go.

The whole let-me-show-you-what-I-can-do-for-you problem was something I had to overcome in my own early interactions with prospects. I'll wager that it's something every successful salesperson has had to address, in one way or another, at some point in his or her career.

You are lucky to work in what I believe is the single most exciting profession on the face of the earth. No matter what it is you sell to other people—pocket calculators, insurance, training services, credit cards, high-level consulting services, automobiles, telecommunications services, whatever—you have a job that is limited only by your own imagination and your own willingness to commit to improve yourself. And no matter what you sell or how you sell it, those two weapons, your imagination and your ability to challenge yourself to improve, can help you overcome any obstacle.

I do mean any obstacle. The one we're discussing now, the powerful initial instinct to try to show the prospect exactly what we can do to him or her, seems daunting the first time you try to mount an attack on it. But guess what? This common obstacle can actually turn into an advantage. By using this book to overcome it, you will separate yourself from 98 percent of the other salespeople contacting your prospects!

That's right. Simply by opening this book and reading this far and by taking the crucial first step toward understanding the obstacles that you may face in your dealings with prospects, you've placed yourself at a significant competitive advantage. You are now familiar with the question-asking pattern that causes the majority of prospects who don't buy, but should, to tune out during your meetings. With extremely rare exceptions, the people you'll be competing against don't know what that pattern looks like. You're now in a position to adjust your approach and become far, far more efficient in your dealings with prospects. They're not. That's quite an accomplishment, don't you agree?

The Myth of "The Need"

Surprise! The customer doesn't "need" you, your product, or your company. In sales, your job is to find out:

1. What the customer is doing;
2. How the customer is doing it;
3. When and where the customer is doing it;
4. Why the customer is doing it;
5. Who the customer is doing it with; and
6. Whether you can help the customer do it better.

Those are the six basic questions we'll be taking on in this book. They do not address issues of whether the customer needs what you have to offer. For most salespeople, this series of questions represents a significant strategic change. Change is sometimes scary, but it is often essential if you hope to progress in your career.

Warning: The above list is not a roadmap for "closing a sale"; neither is it a checklist to be ticked off item-by-item during your initial visit with the prospect. The list you see above is a summary of the important pieces of information you'll need to gather as you develop (or strengthen) a relationship with someone who does business with your company. The six questions show up in a wide variety of settings and at various points in time as your sales develop. Asking them and asking them properly is more of an art than a science, but rest assured that it is an art that can be learned, and in short order. The more proficient you are at knowing when to ask one of these questions, knowing what form to ask it in, and knowing how to follow up on the answer you receive, the more successful you will be in your sales work. That's my promise to you.

Who Really Knows Best?

Before we proceed to an examination of each of the questions, let me ask you something. Do you feel a little uneasy about the notion of assessing your sales work without first addressing the subject of the prospect's "need" for what you are offering? Does learning that this program rejects the entire concept of "need" leave you feeling abandoned somehow?

If you feel uncertain about the prospect of conducting your sales work without focusing on the prospect's "needs," believe me, you're not alone in that regard. Most of the salespeople I train feel exactly the same way at first. Now, don't get me wrong. "Filling the need" certainly sounds like a commendable, selfless type of objective. Somehow, in the execution, though, that doesn't always come off as entirely altruistic. Think of Alice's presentation. She knew there exists a need for the system she was proposing for my company, but she thought (and I emphasize: thought) that the system would perform as successfully in my organization is it had in any number of others. She was wrong.

There's another problem connected with the whole "find the need" approach. If the prospect "needed" what you have to offer, wouldn't he have gone out and gotten it already?

When you think about it, the whole notion of telling the prospective customer what he or she needs is more than a little arrogant. No matter how politely, how professionally, how persuasively we make the "find the need" approach, it still suggests the following thought process on our part:

Step One: I, the salesperson, familiarize myself with a solution to a problem my organization has identified as being connected to a certain group of people. This is a solution that some customers embrace and purchase—or seem to me to be highly likely to embrace and purchase.

Step Two: You, my unwitting future customer, are in need of a solution, although because you haven't done the research on the question that my organization and I have, you may not yet be aware of it.

Step Three: Thanks to some more superior research on my part, I track you down, identify the hole that you have failed to fill without me, and persuade you to implement the solution I've developed.

Conclusion: If all this works, then there was a need. If it doesn't, then there wasn't.

I may be setting things out a little too starkly here—then again, I may not. You have no idea how many tens of thousands of opportunities salespeople have lost by following this approach. The good news is this: You don't have to lose any more of your opportunities this way. Persuading people of the intelligence of implementing what you have to offer has any number of serious drawbacks. The first and most important of these is the real killer. It makes me shake my head in wonder every time I hear some authoritative-sounding sales trainer expounding on the many benefits of "filling the need" during your initial contact with the prospect. Here is the drawback:

You can't address anything vaguely resembling a true need at the outset of the sales cycle because you don't know anything about the prospect yet!

As we've already noted, the great mass of salespeople really don't know about their potential customers. They want to squeeze them into one of those predetermined slots. Once you finish this book, however, you won't have to take your place among those salespeople anymore.

In the next chapter, we will look at each of the six basic types of questions in a little more detail. We'll see what aspect of "doing" each addresses, and we'll examine the basics of the sales cycle you and your prospect will be working through. We'll also review some fundamentals of questioning technique, and we'll explore some simple, but highly effective ideas for posing questions, ideas you'll be using throughout the book.

Chapter Three

The Six Basic Questions and the Objectives Behind Them

Each of the six question areas we reviewed in the previous chapter can produce specific questions; each of these questions can be targeted, focused, phrased, and sequenced in a variety of ways. Look at the list again:

Question Group #1: What the prospect does.

Question Group #2: How the prospect does that.

Question Group #3: When and where the prospect does what he or she does.

Question Group #4: Why the prospect does it that way.

Question Group #5: Who the prospect is currently working with.

Question Group #6: (Advanced—only ask after you've addressed numbers one through five) Whether and how you can help the client do what he or she does better.

Questions in each of these six groups have a specific objective that will not vary, no matter how you decide to structure the question.

In later chapters of this book we'll see a number of specific examples showing how you can link these six powerful questions to the specifics of your prospect's current operation and to the particular individual you're dealing with (as opposed to the organization). Before we get to that, however, we need to look at each of these six questions in depth and explore the unique objective behind each.

Question Number One: What Do You Do?

Variations on Question Number One are meant to determine the nature of the organization's fundamental business goals or the kind of job the person you're speaking to performs. Even if you believe the prospect is engaged in a business with which you feel you're familiar, the truth of the matter is that—at least at the outset of your relationship—you're not familiar with the unique challenges, opportunities, crises, and compromises that this particular prospect faces on a daily basis. You don't yet know about the organization's history, the typical profiles of its target customers, or the level of success or failure it has achieved in reaching and satisfying those customers. Similarly you don't yet know about the career path of a particular contact you've hooked up with, his or her position of influence within the organization, or the specific way his or her job relates to the personal and business goals, formal or informal, that we all strive to achieve on some level.

Here's how you can identify questions that fall into this category:

- When a question is directed toward your contact's everyday business activities or essential business objectives, or focuses on what the people in the organization are trying to accomplish in the grand scheme of things . . .
- When a question seeks to unearth the specifics of why people show up for work every morning, and how they are rewarded for doing what they do . . .
- When a question points toward your contact's personal, career, or business goals . . .

. . . then it is a variation on Question Number One.

Question Number Two: How Do You Do It?

Variations on Question Number Two are meant to determine the means the organization uses to attain its essential business objectives. These questions also serve to cast light on what tactics an individual prospect uses to reach personal goals in a business or career context. Even if you believe the prospect is using a system or service that is similar to those of your other customers, and even if you know that the customer is currently buying a certain product to achieve a particular aim, the truth of the matter is, at least at the beginning of your relationship, you're not familiar with the specific applications or product uses this customer has implemented or rejected. You don't yet know about the organization's past experiments in finding effective ways to attain important objectives. You don't yet know what benchmarks are in place or being contemplated, nor do you know what product-related or system-related successes and failures the organization has experienced. Similarly, you don't yet know about the methods your contact has found (or rejected) when it comes to attaining success or fulfillment on the job. As the relationship with your prospect begins, you do not yet know what broad conclusions his or her company has reached when it comes to determining suitable means for attaining important personal or organizational goals.

To see what questions are in this category:

- When a question is directed toward the way in which your contact pursues essential business objectives . . .
- When a question seeks to unearth the specifics of how people attain, have attained, or plan to attain personal or organizational goals . . .
- When a question points toward your contact's unique experience base, or explores the specifics behind the implementation of particular solutions to certain pressing problems . . .

. . . then it is a variation on Question Number Two.

Question Number Three: When and Where Do You Do It?

Variations on Question Number Three cover a great deal of ground. They are meant to determine the time frame and physical location of the target organization's operations. Is the business strongly affected by seasonal patterns, or does it operate year-round at essentially the same level? Is a particular element of the business something the company is just introducing, or has it been a mainstay of the organization's operation for some time? Does the organization operate out of a single location, or are there a number of branch offices or satellite facilities? Is the organization highly centralized, with all the initiatives either coming from or subject to the approval of a headquarters office? Or is the target organization a more autonomous unit of a larger operation? Even if the structure, business patterns, and overall business profile of the target company strongly suggest to you that it is similar in all essential respects to existing customers, you must determine the specifics for this unique organization. As your relationship with the new prospects begins, you don't yet know enough about the organization's physical facilities, the timing issues it faces, or the youth or age of the division or company with which you are dealing to draw any conclusions.

For this category:

- When a question is directed toward the physical location, yearly business patterns, or youth or age of the division for the company you are targeting . . .
- When a question seeks to unearth the specifics of your contact's personal work history . . .
- When a question points you toward dates, places, and schedules . . .

. . . then it is a variation on Question Number Three.

Question Number Four: Why Do You Do It That Way?

Variations on Question Number Four are meant to cast a light on the priorities and decision making process at that target organization, either on the group or individual level. Even if you believe that their decision making process is substantially similar to that of other customers of yours, you do not, at the outset of your relationship, know how the person you're dealing with—or the organization he or she represents—makes decisions. You don't yet know about the organization's formal and informal lines of authority, its corporate culture, or the degree to which the target organization embraces a group-oriented or individualistic style of problem resolution or purchasing. Similarly, you don't yet know about the individual contact's predisposition when it comes to making decisions or approving purchases—if, indeed, he or she is authorized to approve purchases at all.

An important note: When properly asked, many Type Four questions do not sound like direct queries for information on the topic of decision making authority or organizational purchasing patterns! They must be constructed and delivered with a certain care and subtlety if they are to yield meaningful information. We'll cover the phrasing of this potentially tricky question category later in the book.

For this category:

- When a question is meant to illuminate your contact's or your target organization's typical decision making patterns or list of priorities . . .
- When a question seeks to unearth the specifics of how past or present purchase decisions were made or what changes are anticipated with regard to the authority for making purchasing decisions . . .
- When a question points toward your contact's likely position in the decision making hierarchy at the target organization . . .

. . . then it is a variation on Question Number Four.

Question Number Five: Who Are You Doing It With?

Variations on Question Number Five are meant to help you determine whether another independent supplier is currently working with your target organization and, if so, which one. Even if you have done extensive library research or personally purchased or used the target organization's product or service, and therefore feel you have a reliable indication as to what vendors the organization is using, you must resolve the issue definitively. For instance, the target organization may have a recent problem with a longstanding vendor and may have severed all ties with them within the last forty-eight hours! Alternatively, an organization about which you have no information could be handling all its work in-house and may not be aware of the advantages (or disadvantages!) of working with an outside vendor. As you begin to establish a business relationship with your prospect, you don't yet know the specifics of these issues, and you *must*. Similarly, you don't yet know about the personal sense of loyalty (or lack thereof) that the contact with whom you are meeting holds toward a current vendor.

With this category:

- When a question is directed toward your contact's current relationship with a completing vendor (if any) . . .
- When a question seeks to clarify what kinds of business-to-business alliances, if any, already exist at your target organization and how strong those alliances are . . .
- When a question aims to establish your contact's personal level of loyalty toward a particular vendor . . .

. . . then it is a variation on Question Number Five.

Question Number Six: How Can We Help You Do It Better?

Warning! This is an advanced questioning category. It usually should not be posed before you have developed enough information by means of Questions One through Five. Variations on Question

Number Six are meant to elicit the organization's or prospect's input in developing your formal proposal or to help finalize the implementation of that proposal. Yes, you read that right: In the best case, you will not write or otherwise dictate the proposal outlining what you can do for the prospect. Your aim is going to be to allow the target organization to become the source of the information you deliver when it comes time to "make a pitch." You're going to do this because winning specific input to the content of your proposal, often through posing Group Six questions, will win buy-in on the part of the prospect, and it will substantially increase the likelihood that the product or service you deliver will meet the organization's specifications exactly. By the same token, you will use Group Six questions to find out how you can build long-term person-to-person alliances by helping your contact attain the career or performance goals that matter most to him or her. Please note that Group Six questions include questions that, in other programs, might be considered "closing questions." However, these questions are not aggressive, manipulative, or misleading, as typical "get-the-order" questions so often seem to be.

A typical Group Six question designed to finalize the sale is posed only after you and the prospect have worked together to develop a detailed proposal. Such questions typically sound like this: "So what do you think?" or "Where do you think we should go from here?" or "How do you think we should get started?"

With questions of this type:

- When a question is directed toward getting members of the target company to offer their own feedback on how what you have to offer might best be put to use in their organization . . .
- When a question seeks to clarify what will and won't work in your formal proposal—or seeks to develop an explicit set of commitments from both partners for future activity together . . .
- When a question encourages the prospect to talk about specifically how your two organizations can work in tandem (i.e., "close the sale") . . .

. . . then it is a variation on Question Number Six.

Those are the six most important questions you can ask in your interaction with prospects. As we proceed through this book, we'll be looking at a great many specific questions that are targeted toward particular circumstances. Each time we discuss a specific sales question, I'll let you know which type of question is under discussion. Please allow me to reinforce one critical idea. In doing so, I realize that I risk overemphasizing the point, but believe me, it's one that definitely warrants repetition. Take a moment now to review briefly these six categories we just reviewed. Don't reread them, but do scan them to strengthen the main objective contained within each. Do this now and then come back to this part of the book.

Beware of "Closing Maneuvers"

Why should I ask you to make such a drastic change? Why should I suggest that you develop a "second sense" that will help you determine, in an instant, which of the six categories you should be pursuing at any given moment? Why should I ask you to automatically eliminate any question that doesn't fit into one of the above categories?

The answer is simple. Habit. Earlier in the book we talked about how strong the instinct is to "tell the prospect what we can do" during an initial sales call. After all, we think to ourselves, we're there for a reason, and the reason should have something to do with our product or service, shouldn't it? So what on earth would be more natural or appropriate than to launch into a discussion of how that product or service can benefit the prospect?

I've found, particularly during the final stages of the sale, that this thought process is an extremely seductive one. It's also lightning fast. It stakes its claim on your tongue faster than you can imagine. Even salespeople who have successfully incorporated the ideas I'm talking about in this book find that they must occasionally fight the instinct to talk first about themselves and their company. And most of the salespeople I train find that it takes a great deal of work to make the first meeting move from the "need-based" mindset to the "do-based" mindset. (Of course, the many shortsighted "need-based" sales training programs out there, the ones I imagine had a great deal to do with Alice's perfectly executed crash-and-burn maneuver in my office, don't help matters much.)

Because I'm committed to helping you move to the next level, the optimum level in your sales career, I'm asking you to make an agreement with yourself here and now to ask only questions that fall into one of the six categories I've just outlined (or into the minor "pleasantry" subcategory we'll discuss a little later) during your sales calls and visits. More specifically, I want you to abandon, for good, the notion that "closing" the sale is a mysterious specialized activity that is somehow separate from the rest of the process. Too often we convince ourselves that "closing" is a special method of persuasion for manipulation that the "strong" salespeople manage to exert on their prospects, and that "weak" salespeople do not. Once you have made these agreements, you will be in a perfect position to take advantage of what the rest of this book has to offer.

I'm emphasizing this point so strongly because there are a great many potentially career-destroying ideas out there about "how to close the sale." The way I see it, most of them are directly connected to the "need-based" philosophy of selling. That school's vaunted "closing tactics" demonstrate, as vividly as any other aspect of the "need-based" approach, how ineffective this type of selling really is. Those tactics are taught—and, all too often, followed—because they promise us that we don't have to think about things from the prospect's point of view before we suggest something. We can just toss off a one-size-fits-all "closing line" to each and every person we run into and then stand back and count the commissions as they roll in. It's a lie and perhaps the most dangerous lie of the whole "need-based" sales technique.

Just Say "No, Thank You"

Some closing maneuvers, supposedly designed to win you sales, are so absurd that not only will they earn you a reputation as a pushy salesperson, but they are also likely to brand you as a completely inept one. If anyone suggests that you use any of the following techniques, just say, "Thanks, but no thanks."

Consider, for instance the "pen-rolling close," in which you're supposed to complete your pitch, wait for the appropriate moment when the prospect is "open to suggestion" (or some other pseudo-scientific mumbo-jumbo), and then, out of the blue, roll your pen across the desk. When the surprised prospect picks it up, you're supposed to say something along these lines, "Well, now that you've got the pen in your hand, why not just sign here on the dotted line? Press hard, you're making three copies, okay?" I trust you agree that those are not the most effectively phrased sales questions you can pose.

I wish I could say that I was making up such advice, but I'm not. Some sales trainer out there actually expects you to pull this stunt. When you think about it, is flinging a pen at your prospect any more out of step with the person's true interests than to simply repeat the text of the brochure you brought along and insist that the model it describes is what he or she needs, as Alice did?

Unfortunately, the parade of dumb advice doesn't end with that rolling of the pen across the table. There's also the "self-pity close," in which you are supposed to look the prospect straight in the eye and say, "Mr. Jones, if you don't buy from me, I'm going to lose my job. Can we please ship you twelve gross of the Model X widget?"

I have also heard sales trainers advocate the "Mama always said" close. For this one, you're supposed to wait for a pause in the conversation and then deliver this line: "You know, my dear white-haired mother always used to say that silence was really the same thing as consent. So why don't we just ship you the twelve gross of the Model X widget?"

Also making the rounds is the "puppy-dog close." This does not, despite its name, involve bringing along to your meeting a small, adorable dog that's about to be sent to the pound—and then pleading for the sale on the theory that, if only you had a little more money to spend in your household, you wouldn't have to give up your pet. (Given the ridiculousness of some of the ideas being espoused these days, though, I wouldn't be too surprised to see even that variation earn support from some of the "need-based" sales trainers out there.) No, under the "puppy-dog" close, the idea is to recite the many wonderful advantages of using your product and then announce that you're leaving it back on-site for two weeks at no charge. Never mind how, or when, or how often, or whether the prospect will use the product in the first place. Never mind the prospect's past in using such products. Never mind the present challenges the prospect is facing. Simply ask, "Would you mind if I left the twelve gross of widgets here for two weeks so you can try them out, Mr. Jones?"

Then there's the "Ben Franklin close," in which you suggest to the prospect that the two of you list the advantages of buying from you on one side of the sheet of paper and the disadvantages on the other side. As you do so, you say something like this: "Mr. Jones, if you come up with more disadvantages than I can come up with advantages, I will walk out of that door right now and I won't bother you again. But if my advantages outnumber your disadvantages, then I win, and we ship you the twelve gross of the Model X widget. That sounds fair, doesn't it?" This is one of my favorite examples of idiotic person-to-person selling. I have seen it in action firsthand and have heard sales reps tell me that they want me to engage in a game in which I buy their product if they "win"! Presumably, the rep's product was supposed to constitute my punishment if I "lost."

All those ideas are, quite frankly, laughable. But they're laughable only because they're usually bad at camouflaging the fact that they leave the prospect out of the equation. Like hundreds of less blatantly stupid techniques out there (techniques taught by people who should know better), these "closing maneuvers" attempt to fit the prospect into a predetermined mold. They ignore the unique situations he or she faces. But you know what? They're very seductive.

I think I know why they're seductive, too. Deep down, we'd all like to believe that top-level selling can work in a way the "need-based" school would lead us to believe it does. We'd like to believe that something magical would work, because asking more meaningful questions can sometimes be a little unfamiliar and therefore a little intimidating—at first! What we don't know is always more intimidating than what we do know. We'd all like to believe that we can progress through the sales cycle, not by addressing things we aren't sure of, but by addressing things we are sure of—in other words, by asking questions to which we know (or think we know) the answers. We'd all like to believe that a few simple key words, deftly phrased by the experts and read verbatim at a certain predetermined point in the meeting, can turn a prospect into a customer.

I'm here to tell you that if you want to reach your true potential as a salesperson, you have to find another way. It's probably obvious to you that each of the questions in all these so-called "closing maneuvers" we've just reviewed would fail, in an instant, the test I've suggested— the one that incorporates reviewing what you plan to ask against the six-category model. I hope you're beginning to see, too, how that model will help you avoid following similarly misguided, but less transparently foolish advice from the "need-based" school of selling.

What's in a Name?

There are many names for the kind of selling that my six-point model, when followed, seeks to replace. I call it "need-based" selling, but you'll also find sales trainers who talk about "tactical" selling, or "turn-around-oriented" selling, or selling that "finds the pain," or selling that "focuses on interpersonal keys." There are probably a hundred different variations of the Big Sales Lie that I'm trying to help you eradicate with this program. Whatever you call these many approaches, they are all systems that proceed from the assumption that you know most of the essentials about the prospect from the get-go, and that questioning or interviewing is essentially a tool for establishing some form of control over him or her. That's a critical error, and it's one I have developed the six-point model to help you avoid.

In the next chapter, we'll take a look at your potential prospect base—and see precisely why effective questioning can help you make the most of it.

Chapter Four

Silver, Bronze, and Gold

Before we proceed any further, let me ask you: Have you made your own personal commitment to work within the six-category model outlined in the previous chapter when it comes to asking your prospective questions? If you haven't, let me warn you one final time that the temptations to "dump" on the prospect or to ask questions designed to exert control rather than obtain information are very strong ones indeed. Sadly, a great many salespeople engage in these techniques . . . some even after they know full well the harm it can cause to their careers. Don't be one of them.

The program this book will outline is not one that can be incorporated into your routine halfway. It's an all-or-nothing proposition. If you simply skim what follows for ideas you can incorporate into an approach that still reverts, by design or by instinct, to that terrifically strong impulse to "tell the prospect what you can do for him," you will be wasting your time by continuing with this book.

Get the very most that you can from what follows; make a resolution right now to follow the six-category model for each and every question you pose to the prospect.

The Margin of Victory

I'd like you to take a moment to think back to the last Olympic speed-skating, swimming, or track and field event you watched on television.

In these high-speed, high-energy contests, the margin of victory between the person who comes in first and the person who comes in second is often infinitesimal. In the 100-meter dash, for instance, the gold medal winner often posts a time that is only tenths, or even hundredths, of a second better than those of his two nearest rivals. Stop and think for a moment about exactly how long twelve-hundredths of a second actually is. It's about as long as it takes you to blink your eyes once.

Even so, that twelve-hundredths of a second interval, that time it takes you to blink, can mean the difference between worldwide acclaim and a sports page footnote. There's nothing wrong with a silver medal in the abstract, of course, but we are much more likely to shower media coverage, endorsement contracts, and superstar status on the winner. On that person who establishes a twelve-hundredths of a second margin over the competition.

My point is not that we spend too much time focusing on the winners of athletic contests, although that may well be the case, but that in some instances, tiny margins of victory can carry immense implications. That's the way it is with sales, too. The actual performance differences between top-level salespeople and those in the tier below them are, at least in theory, quite modest. But the differences are there, as are some fairly dramatic increases in the rewards for the top performers.

My own perception of the events like the speedskating or swimming competition yields another interesting comparison with the world of sales. It seems to me that in those types of contests, the numerical differences between the performances of those at or near the bottom of the field tends to be greater than in those hairsbreadth finishes we usually associate with the top competitors in the race. The person who comes in ninth or tenth or thirtieth often doesn't finish a scant fraction of the second ahead of or behind the next participant, but instead perhaps three, four, or ten seconds between himself and that competitor. Similarly, in sales work, there seems to be a whole lot of ways to struggle along and barely hang in there.

So what have we got? The competition to enter, say, the top third of salespeople—the sales elite, if you will—is quite intense and is marked by fairly narrow distinctions in levels of performance. We might even connect the entry to the top-third level to the unending refinements the people who are posting the very best results make, the ongoing commitment they show to getting a little more information about their prospects and customers. At the other end of the scale, the bottom third, there's not as much of this type of innovation, and there's a much wider performance-level pattern.

I realize that it might seem that I'm pushing this parallel with the world of sports a little too far. I mention it because it reflects an important principle you'll need to take advantage of if you want to make the most of your potential as a salesperson.

As it turns out, effective use of the six questions we reviewed in the previous chapter allows you to broaden your appeal to the largest number of prospects you can expect to reach, to make the most of the time available to you, and to have the best chance of establishing business relationships with those prospects. As I see it, becoming intimately familiar with the six main questions and their innumerable variations is one of the key refinements that you can expect to help you win entry into the top tier of sales performers. In and of themselves, working with the questions may look like a fairly modest undertaking but doing so consistently and perfecting your technique carries significant rewards. By contrast, "following our instincts" or "doing what's worked for us before" is probably more representative of the bottom third of the finishers at the race—the third that doesn't take advantage of innovation for refinement as effectively.

Who Could Buy from You?

Let's look at this (admittedly complex) idea in another way. Think for a moment about a set of people—that group of people who could conceivably decide to buy what we have to offer over the next twelve months.

The group we're talking about doesn't just consist of all those people who are likely to buy from us in the next year. It's all the people we could conceivably sell to in a perfect world if every decision went our way. Obviously, the group doesn't include people outside our possible customer base. If we're selling training sessions on how to learn to speak Italian, people who are already fluent in Italian aren't going to pay to take them.

I don't know exactly how many people we're talking about, and the odds are that you don't know either. But that doesn't much matter.

The specific number isn't the issue. What is important is grasping the idea of our total potential prospect base. We're going to take this group of people, which consists of all the sales we could conceivably close over the next twelve months, and we're going to refer to that unknown figure, that imaginary gathering of as-yet-unsold prospects, as X.

If everything I do, and I mean everything, went our way over the next twelve months, we could close X sales. Now let's look a little more closely at the types of buyers included in that figure of X. Yes, we can do some extrapolating, and we can draw some important insights on that group, even without hard numbers. My twenty-seven years as a sales trainer and my training sessions and interviews with over a quarter of a million real, live salespeople lead me to propose the following rough breakdown of our total potential prospect base. Roughly a third of that group is almost certainly going to buy from us simply because we showed up, called, or knocked on the door. This group makes up what I call the right-place/right-time sales. The specifics of all we have to offer—the performance, the price, the perceived value, and the turnaround time, whatever—happened to match exactly what the organization is looking for. This "easy" third, by the way, is the third that allows "need-based" selling programs to thrive. The prospects in this group are the people who, by sheer happenstance, do need something like the Expanding Outlet Scale System Alice was so excited about. It happens to match the technical requirements their people are looking for. It happens to correspond, more or less, with the budget their top management has approved. And Alice happens to have landed on their doorstep at a time when they're considering switching systems or are at least open to the idea. So Alice gets a sale from this group. If Alice reaches all the people in this third of the prospect base over the course of the next year, odds are she'll make sales to all of them. (She wouldn't be guaranteed to do so, of course, since a lousy presentation can torpedo even the sale that descends from the heavens, but most of these opportunities would take a good deal of work to mess up.)

Whether Alice can keep these customers for a year is an open question, since she doesn't, as a general rule, know enough about the people who use what she has to offer to hold out much hope of developing anything like a long-term alliance with them. But unless she is openly hostile to her contacts or otherwise completely inept,

Alice will ring up and earn commissions on the vast majority of these right-time/right-place sales.

The middle third of the potential prospect base is not, in the final analysis, going to buy from us, no matter what we do. Although, as the year begins, prospects in this group have a statistical possibility of becoming a customer, as the year unfolds, events are going to make it impossible for them to decide to purchase. Halfway through the year, for instance, a prospect in this group may face a crippling defect, such a product recall that forces them to move into crisis mode and postpone all new purchases in our area indefinitely. Perhaps a competitor will beat us to the punch and establish a long-term contract with one of these prospects. Perhaps a potential customer will become involved in a major antitrust lawsuit that finally results in a multibillion-dollar settlement, placing that company under severe cash constraints. Whatever the reasons, members of this third of the prospect end up answering "no" because of something unforeseen that occurs during the year, and that "no" is not one we can expect to turn around.

The final third of the prospect base is the one the Alices of the world mismanage so tragically. It contains those customers who could go either way when it comes to buying from us. In Alice's case, this group would probably have included my company. Her failure to search effectively for even the most elemental information about what my firm did kept her from winning a shot at installing the phone system. Sadly, her poor questioning technique is all too common among today's salespeople, and most reps do not get the results they should out of this final third of the prospect base.

Go for the Medal You Deserve

To me, salespeople who focus exclusively or primarily on the first third of the prospect base, the one that results in right-place/right-time sales, are a little reminiscent of a speed skater who finishes in third place, thirty seconds behind the winner. I call such salespeople bronze medal winners.

Salespeople who close all the first-third sales, but who have also begun to discover the incredible advantages that proper questioning can give them when it comes to making the most of their relationships with final-third prospects, are like a racer who has really started to hit his stride. These salespeople aren't yet at maximum effectiveness, because overcoming old "need-based" habits is a tough job that takes a while to complete. But they are beginning to respond by instinct in an efficient, "do-based" method to all the prospects they meet, and their results show it. They remind me of the speed skater who finishes in second place, just a hundredth of a second behind the gold medal winner. I call such salespeople silver medal winners.

Finally, salespeople who are, as a general rule, working at full efficiency to convert the sales in the right-place/right-time category and the could-go-either-way category, salespeople who are building long-term alliances, are like a racer who noses out the tough competition at the ribbon. I call such salespeople gold medal winners. And you can be one of them.

Chapter Five

The Sales Cycle

Every sale you initiate can be broken down into four, chronological segments. Sometimes the segments follow one another with breathtaking speed during a single telephone exchange; sometimes they're stretched out over a period of months or even years! It all depends on the industry within which you work, the type of customer you typically work with, and the specific business objectives of your prospect. Nevertheless, each of the four phases of the sale (which I call the sales cycle) marks a separate, unique portion of your emerging relationship with your potential customer.

Although many salespeople sell "on instinct" quite effectively without ever breaking down their sales cycle or recognizing its component parts, it's a valuable exercise to review the four phases of the sale closely. Doing so will certainly help you get the most out of this program. Here, then, is a brief summary of the four phases of the sales cycle.

Phase One: Prospecting

In most cases, the prospecting phase of the sale corresponds with the oft-postponed task, the cold call. (I've been saying for years that when God decided that it was time to punish salespeople, he invented the cold call!)

Actually, prospecting can—and often does—take place through any number of alternate methods, including third party referrals, fax transmissions requesting a return call, or even showing up unannounced at the prospect's door. In all cases, though, the prospecting phase is when we find out whether there's a reason for further discussion about the product or service we offer.

During the prospecting phase, we're not, of course, concerned with determining whether the person we're contacting "needs" what we are selling. And we're certainly not trying at this stage to get a formal commitment to buy. We're making an exploratory inquiry, typically with the sole aim of setting up an in-person appointment.

Prospecting in general, and effective telephone prospecting in particular, can be the most important sales tool at your disposal. Space prevents me from offering a detailed analysis of the many steps you can take to get the most out of your telephone prospecting efforts, but I would like to pass along the following basic telephone script, which is a variation on one I have used with great success in my seminars (and to develop new business for my own company!) for many years.

A good cold call should sound something like this:

Prospect: Hello?

You: Hello, Mr. Jones. This is James Brown from ABC Corporation here in Chicago.

Once you reach the person you're after (or believe to be a likely decision maker) limit the opening statement to something along the lines I've just outlined. Don't ask how the prospect's doing, whether he's got any time, whether you can talk to him for a moment, whether he has a headache, or anything else. Simply say hello and make the statement. Then briefly state the point of your call (which is to get an appointment) and the benefits of your product or service, and conclude with a nonthreatening statement or question the prospect may choose to agree with. Don't use a yes-or-no-oriented question; the contact will supply you with whichever answer will get you off the phone.

You: I've wanted to get in touch with you, Mr. Jones, to introduce you to our sales training service, which can help you increase your sales performance by as much as 40 percent. I'm sure that you, like XYZ Company, are interested in improving the results in your sales department.

If the prospect responds affirmatively, conclude by setting the appointment:

You: That's great, Mr. Jones. Let's get together so we can talk about this in a little more detail. How about Tuesday at one?

Don't offer alternative times. If the time you suggest isn't good for the prospect, let him tell you.

If Mr. Jones offers an objection for response like this . . .

Mr. Jones: Sales training is too expensive (or doesn't deliver long-term results) (or is something we handle in-house) (or anything else that isn't an outright rejection, but rather a masked expression of interest).

. . . don't panic! I always give the response/objection the attention it deserves by responding with this (entirely accurate!) assessment of what my company offers:

You: You know, Mr. Jones, that's what a lot of companies who ended up doing business with us said to me before they had the chance to see the benefits of our program. ABC Pharmaceuticals, a company I did a program with just a few months back, told me they wanted to stay with their in-house training program. As it turned out, they were very happy with our program, and they noticed a 30 percent increase in sales revenue as a result of our techniques. I'd really like to get together with you to talk about this—how's Tuesday at one?

You can adapt this very effective objection response to your own industry easily, inserting success stories of your own. It should go without saying—but for the sake of thoroughness I'll include the point here—that you must never exaggerate or overstate what your organization has done for a customer!

Suppose Mr. Jones tells you he doesn't want to improve the results of his sales department. Thank him politely, say goodbye, and move on to the next call. Pressuring the prospect at this stage or trying to get him to admit the pointlessness of his statement will only invite conflict and force you to waste energy. End the conversation.

Although some telemarketing salespeople compress their sales cycle in such a way that commitments to buy result from an initial call, most of us who use prospecting calls to set up appointments have a different agenda. Prospecting calls are typically not meant to result in an agreement to buy your product or service. They usually occupy a very small portion of any given sales cycle. Let's face it: Either the person wants to talk to you or he doesn't.

Just as a side note, let me mention here that I am one sales trainer who practices exactly what he preaches. Every single business day that I'm not out on the road, I make fifteen calls using this script I've just outlined. Of those fifteen calls, I make contact with seven decision makers. And as a result of talking to those seven decision makers, I set up one new appointment. Of all the appointments that lead to full-sales presentations, I close eight out of ten sales. Those numbers, which I monitor closely and continuously (just as you should) reflect a day-in, day-out routine with me. Prospecting via cold calling may be considered "drudge work" by some, but those of us whose careers have been based on solid cold selling habits know that it is a critical element of the sales cycle. If you choose to ignore it to focus on "current business," you do so at your own peril! (And watch out when the empty pipeline greets you a few months after you decide to take it easy on the prospecting.)

Phase Two: Interviewing

Interviewing typically consists of face-to-face meetings with one or more representatives of the target company you identified through your prospecting efforts. The purpose of the interviewing stage is to gather information about the aims of the prospect and his company. Interviewing can proceed in a logical sequence focusing on past experiences, current projects, and future plans, or it can focus on whatever sequence of events makes the most sense to the prospect. For the sake of clarity, we're going to examine an interviewing stage set up in roughly chronological order. The vast majority of what you'll be reading about in subsequent chapters deals with the interviewing stage.

An important note: Failure to devote enough time to the interviewing stage is one of the chief distinguishing characteristics of bronze medal salespeople! The interviewing stage is meant to allow you to find out all relevant information with regard to the target company's—and the prospect's personal—history, current challenges, and objectives for the future. That is not the same thing as finding out whether he or she has an immediate application for a particular product or for a particular aspect of your service.

My own estimate is that you should expect to spend approximately 75 percent of the total time of any given sales cycle in the interviewing phase. This means that you're not trying to sell during the first three quarters—at least—of your relationship with the prospect. Naturally this estimate will vary from industry to industry and depending upon the particular requirements of the individual prospect. But the figure is a good benchmark to keep in mind all the same.

The interviewing phase, which is the main focus of this book, is where most of your real work takes place. It's where you verify that you were right in your assumptions about how the project might be able to use what you have to offer. It's where you find out whether you have to change course with regard to what you eventually propose to the prospect—and how you need to change course. The key to verifying and changing course is the intelligent application of the six basic questions.

In our sales model, the only selling that takes place is selling that makes sense to the prospect first. If the interviewing phase of the sales cycle is conducted correctly, all pertinent issues are explored thoroughly and from the prospect's point of view.

Phase Three: Presentation

This is the point of the sale where you formalize your recommendation and spell out exactly what it is you feel you can offer the prospect. Typically, you'll also identify the time frame within which you and the prospect can expect to work, and you'll give your contact an accurate idea of how much it will then cost to achieve the results or resolve the problems you've been discussing.

As I mentioned earlier, the best part about the presentation phase is that this is when, in a great many cases, you can expect to get the prospect to help you develop nearly all of the essential details of your formal presentation. I realize that this sounds, at first, like a remarkable or even audacious thing to expect from someone with whom you hope to do business. In fact, however, it's the most natural thing in the world. Remember how eager the executives at Mark's target firm were to share the specifics of "what they were trying to accomplish"? Remember how easy it was for him to schedule a follow-up meeting at which everyone could contribute to a more detailed discussion of the options at the company's disposal? Remember how one of the executives volunteered to schedule the meeting so that the president of the target company could attend?

Mark's story provides us with a dramatic example of how solid questioning can get the prospect to "open up" and help the salesperson develop a formal proposal, but his experience is by no means unique! I've based my own sales career on eliciting the same kind of feedback from prospects, and so have thousands of salespeople who've attended my seminars and training sessions.

The reason this idea works is simple: People like talking about themselves and their problems. When you listen to people, when you ask appropriate questions, and when you follow up by noting appropriate information and returning to a listening mode—instead of using your questions as an excuse to get your own message across—people realize you may actually be able to customize something to their needs. And they often give you all the information you need in order to help you do this.

Presentations typically appear in bound text format; sometimes they take advantage of the snazzy text arrangements and color graphics today's word-processing and graphics programs make possible. Although I would never deny the attention-grabbing power of color and superior page layout, I usually caution salespeople against relying on such tools too heavily. Unless you work for a graphic arts or publishing firm, your aim is not to convince people how wonderful your formal presentation proposal looks, but how effectively it mirrors the concerns and suggestions you noted during the interviewing stage.

Phase Four: Closing

Let me be perfectly honest with you: I hate identifying the final stage of the sales process as "closing," and I heartily wish the sales world would come up with another word. This phrase, which most sales reps (and, perhaps more influentially, their sales managers) refuse to let go of, summons all the wrong images. If it were up to you, would you choose to be "closing," or would you choose to be initiating a potentially lucrative partnership with a new business ally?

I realize, however, that such a formulation is a little cumbersome, and I also realize that we tend, through force of habit as much as anything else, to think of finalizing the sale as "closing" it. In this program, converting the sale is not a matter of coercion or overriding a personality, but is rather a logical progression of all that has gone before. It is a final confirmation that what you and the prospect have developed together does in fact make sense. It's the initiation of a new business relationship on the basis that your in-person research leads you to believe is going to make for a good "fit" with the prospect. You cannot initiate the relationship before the prospect is ready to, any more than one person can, on his or her own, decide to get married.

My favorite way to close a sale is to say something like this to the prospect near the end of the sales cycle:

"So . . . it makes sense to me. What do you think?"
Or:
"Where do you think we should go from here?"
Or:
"How do you want to proceed now?"

As you can see, those aren't magic words designed somehow to turn a "no" into a "yes"—they're intelligent, gentle, appropriate queries meant to get the prospect to take the lead and formalize the relationship. If you've done your work properly up to this point, questions like those are all you will need.

A Dynamic Model

What I've just outlined is a dynamic model, not a static one. You can't (or, at any rate, shouldn't!) be in one phase of the cycle without knowing that you're trying to move the sale forward to the next phase. Accordingly, the goal of the prospecting stage is to complete the prospecting work and progress to the interviewing stage. The goal of the interviewing stage is to complete the interviewing work and move ahead to the presentation stage. (But note that the vast majority of bronze and silver medal salespeople I work with must be relieved of a potentially fatal habit of trying to move forward to presentation before the prospect is ready. And, finally, the goal of the presentation stage is to complete the presentation and close the sale.

I'll wager that the four phases sounded familiar to you as I recounted them. Virtually anyone in my seminars who's done any amount of selling recognizes the four steps and many remark that they'd already been selling according to the model for some time, but had simply never used names to set the four distinct periods apart. As we've seen, setting them apart is crucial. The first and the last phase are, when properly handled, often breathtakingly fast. The two in the middle can each take a long time indeed. Each phase, in the abstract, would seem to be easy enough to distinguish from the other three—yet many a sales rep has tried to present his or her product within seconds of reaching a prospect on the phone or attempted to close shortly after sitting down with the prospect for the first time.

To make the most of your sales potential, you have to know what phase of the cycle you're in. Specifically, with regard to most of the advice on sales questioning techniques that follows in this book, you need to know when you've entered the interviewing phase of the cycle. That, as we have seen, is where most of your work lies, and that's also where you'll be able to use the framing technique we'll be discussing a little later to the best effect.

Chapter Six

The Interviewing Phase: Techniques That Work

How will you be able to tell whether you've made it to the interviewing phase? Typically it's when you sit down face-to-face with your prospect for the first time, after having engaged in a few innocuous questions that fall into the "general question" or "small talk" category.

These questions should not take long. I'm personally very suspicious of sales reps that spend a great deal of time in the small talk phase. Some form of initial pleasantry is of course essential, but I think it's important to bear in mind that, as a general rule, we do live in a let's-get-to-the-heart-of-the-matter society.

Some organizations boast a laid-back culture that encourages extensive "give and take" during the initial greetings stage, but it is my opinion that they're easily outnumbered by firms that would rather dispense with the introductions and the small talk relatively quickly and move on to the reason the meeting is taking place. More than one sales rep I've worked with has had the experience of "building rapport" with the key decision maker and getting that decision maker to open up by telling lots of stories—only to be ordered out of the room before anything of consequence happened because the decision maker had another appointment waiting outside that couldn't be changed!

Innocuous introductory or greeting questions that, as we have noted earlier, did not fall within the six-category model, might sound like the following examples.

> *You:* Mr. Jones, how are you?
> Or:
> *You:* Mr. Jones, it's great to finally meet you. I had a great talk with Alannah outside; is she always that nice?
> Or:
> *You:* Mr. Jones, nice to meet you. How are things going today?

These are essentially "getting-to-know-you" questions; they're very nearly content-free, and they serve to cover the initial few moments in which you and the prospect shake hands, remark on the surroundings, discuss the weather, or otherwise acquaint yourself with one another for the first time. (Note: In the next chapter, we'll see how some questions that sound like small talk can be used to elicit important personal information that could be crucial to your sale. Right now, however, we'll assume that you aren't adding this refinement to your interviewing style and that you're proceeding according to the simplest outline applicable to the interviewing phase.)

For most of us, the interviewing phase begins in earnest after we step into the prospect's office and we've exchanged a few initial pleasantries. Paradoxically, we must often initiate the interviewing phase at that point of the sale that sounds the most like we're being interviewed.

We take a seat, make a little small talk by means of questions like the ones outlined above, and then listen as the prospect says something along these lines:

> *Prospect:* So—what can you do for us?
> Or:
> *Prospect:* Tell me about your program.
> Or:
> *Prospect:* Let's hear about the way you'd structure a seminar for our salespeople.
> Or:
> *Prospect:* Fill me in. I want to hear everything.

These familiar conversation-starters, although they're usually delivered with good humor (or perhaps a display of scrupulously maintained patience in the midst of a busy day), are disasters waiting to happen.

Why? The questions the prospect poses sound so inviting—and they seem like such great openings—that we're usually tempted to tell the person what we can do for him or her. Or provide all the details of our program. Or explain the way we'd arrange a seminar for that kind of company we think we're dealing with. Or explain everything we can think of about our product or service.

For reasons I hope are obvious to you by now, the prospect's invitation to "tell him about the product," as welcome as it may seem, is one we must politely decline. Actually, to be more accurate, we must replace the question with another one, and we must do it in a way that leaves the prospect feeling good about the shift. Here's what it should sound like:

You: Before we start, Mr. Prospect, would it help if I told you a bit about me and my company first?

As you do this, or shortly before you do this, you should extract a notepad and a pen from your briefcase. Even though you're about to give a brief summary about your company, you'll be sending an important visual message by removing that notepad: "I'm here to listen."

Do not ask for permission to take notes. Your aim is to send a nonverbal signal that you are ready to pay attention and ready to do business. The notepad and pen are among the most effective tools a salesperson can employ. In the following pages, we will be talking a great deal about how you can put them to good use.

The simple before-we-get-started question I've just set out is unusual in several respects. For one thing, as the starting point of the interviewing phase, it subtly strips the emphasis from the prospect's typical query about "exactly what do you do" in the current situation to what you and your organization have done in the past. And by the way, in case you were wondering: This inaugural question lays the foundation for all the questions that follow. It does not fall into one of the six categories we discussed earlier in the book, but it is nevertheless mandatory as a starting point.

Posing the above question during the very early part of your post-introduction interaction with the prospect is, in my view, essential. You simply *have* to ask it—that is, assuming you want to get the most you can possibly get from the sales-based interviewing program that is the heart of this book. What's more, I'd strongly urge you to pose it as I have laid it out, without altering it or adapting it in any way. This question has been proven to start relationships off right, so please use it as written.

If you do, you'll be accomplishing a number of important goals. You'll be letting the prospect know in an unthreatening way that it's time to begin the sales call in earnest. You'll be taking a little pressure off the prospect, who is often uneasy about whose job it is to "conduct" the meeting. And you'll be quietly laying the groundwork for the first real fact-gathering questions you will be asking.

What will the prospect say in response? Well, my experience has been that roughly 90 percent of the time, when you ask . . .

You: Before we start, Mr. Prospect, would it help if I told you a little bit about me and my company first?

. . . the prospect will say something like this:

Prospect: Sure, that sounds like a good idea.

Once in a while, you'll run into a prospect that's in a crisis mode. In such cases, you may get an answer along the following lines:

Prospect: No, I think I'd better outline what we're facing here first.

That's fine. Return to your pad and start taking notes. You will essentially be taking part in an accelerated interviewing stage, one in which the prospect moves several steps ahead. The chapters that follow will show you what to ask and when.

No matter what the prospect says, however, you must avoid going into the specifics of what your organization has to offer the prospect's company. You don't yet have enough information to make any meaningful suggestions.

Let's assume, in the present case, that you're dealing with a standard interview, one in which you've asked the initial question in the way I outlined, and the prospect has told you that he or she has no problem with you briefly summarizing your company's work—and your own. You will proceed to deliver an extremely brief, extremely general accounting of your company's history and some indication of your role in the company. It could sound something like this:

> **You:** I'm the president of RabbWorks, a literary agency, freelance writing service, and packaging firm that's done work with such publishers as Prentice Hall, Contemporary Books, McGraw-Hill, and Carol Publishing. We're in our second year of operation, and we're involved in some extremely exciting projects, including a book called **The Accelerated Job Search**, which has just been released to the bookstores.

That's about as long and detailed as you should get: two healthy sentences. Perhaps three at the most. This biography is not an excuse to discourse at length, show off charts and graphs, or engage in one-upmanship. Keep it short and sweet.

The beauty of this brief statement is that it sounds as though it's about to launch into a hard-sell, but it doesn't last long enough to merit an interruption. Instead, it interrupts itself. And when it interrupts itself, it allows you the first opportunity to use an important questioning technique: framing.

Framing

At the end of your brief biography, you're going to ask a straightforward question regarding the prospect's past use, if any, of the type of product or service you handle. Then you're going to follow up the response you get with a question sequence culminating in a special kind of question, one designed to get you contradicted. This type of question is known as a framed question, and you'll be using it often.

I should note here that in posing this framed question, you'll be issuing the first honest-to-goodness information-gathering query of your interaction with the prospect, and you'll be beginning the "what happened in the past" portion of your questioning process. Because your very first question must arise naturally and without fanfare from your introductory biography paragraph, I'm placing it in this chapter rather than the next one.

Let me describe exactly what I mean when I talk about a framed question. I realize it sounds a little strange at first to pose a question that's meant to encourage the prospect to contradict you. At a certain point, you're going to incorporate the specific assumption within the question sequence that points in the opposite direction from the answer you "expect."

Here are some examples of exchanges that result in framed questions. Each shows how you can work toward posing a framed question as you reach the end of your brief company biography.

Example #1:

You: . . . which has just been released to the bookstores. Mr. Jones, before I go any further, I'm just curious. Have you ever met with a book packager before? *[Past-oriented variation on Question Number Five: Who Are You Doing It With?]*

Prospect: Yes. We've done a couple of books with Right-Read Associates.

You: Really? How did working with them go? *[Past-oriented variation on Question Number Two: How Do You Do It?]*

Prospect: They had their problems.

You: Is that so? Gee, I've talked to a lot of people who only had positive things to say about them. What happened? *[Despite the way this question is structured, you actually do know that some of Right Read's customers are unhappy with them! This is a framed, past-oriented version on Question Number Two: How Do You Do It?]*

Prospect: Well, the difficulty was, when it came time to assemble the indexes for the books we signed with them, they claimed that that wasn't covered in their contract. So that was a headache for the production department and the only way it was resolved . . . .

Example #2:

You: DEI Management Group is one of the world's premier sales training organizations. We've worked with firms like AT&T, Motorola, and Cigna, and we're currently branching out into international operations, which is pretty exciting. I just concluded a prospecting training session in London last week. Mr. Jones, before I go any further, I'm just curious. Have you met with a sales training firm or company before? *[Past-oriented variation on Question Number Five: Who Are You Doing It With?]*

Prospect: Yes, we have.

You: What firm did you work with? *[Past-oriented variation on Question Number Five: Who Are You Doing It With?]*

Prospect: It's a little outfit known as Capitol Consulting; you've probably never heard of them.

You: No, you're right, I haven't. So how did the project you were working on with them turn out? What kind of issues did you have to look at? *[Past-oriented variation on Question Number Two: How Do You Do It?]*

Prospect: I'll tell you the truth, I wasn't too crazy about it. This whole meeting today, actually, I should warn you that it's probably something of a shot in the dark for you, because we've basically concluded that sales training really doesn't work for us.

You: Huh. Sounds like you've really had some trouble with this area in the past. So—is Capitol Consulting an out-of-state firm? *[Framed, past-oriented combination of Question Number Five: Who Are You Doing It With? and Question Number Three: When and Where Do You Do It?]*

Prospect: No, no, it's right here in town. In fact, it's operated by the brother-in-law of our CEO. We've done five or six other programs, and we really haven't been able to track any results in our sales performance whatsoever.

Example #3:

You: Chromium Widgets is the largest manufacturer of specialized widget assemblies in the United States. We've been in business since 1961, and we've developed customized widgets for companies like Pop Fellas Consumer Products, Ideal High Fidelity Manufacturing, and Hopponit Bicycles. Lately we've started to develop widgets solutions for smaller start-up firms, too. Mr. Jones, before I go any further, I'm just curious. Do you have a relationship with a widget supplier currently? *[Past-oriented variation on Question Number Five: Who Are You Doing It With?]*

Prospect: Yes, we're working with Johnell Widget.

You: So did you have to put a lot of money up front in order to get things started with them? I've heard from some of the other people in the industry that a lot of companies sometimes ask for that up-front when they're working with a start-up firm. *[Framed, past-oriented variation on Question Number Two: How Do You Do It?]*

Prospect: No, actually they put together a pretty flexible payment plan for us, and I guess I'd have to say that was one of the key reasons we went with them. We needed the widgets in a hurry to meet a shipping date we had coming, and when we met with the rep, he talked about one that would let us . . . .

Did you notice how the framed question, the one that was designed to get the prospect to correct us, resulted in the prospect offering lots of important information for us to write down on our pad? By the way, if the prospect provides you with the information and you don't write it down, go back three spaces and give two hundred dollars worth of Monopoly money to the bank! Writing down the facts shows the prospect that he or she is the most important thing in your universe at that moment in time. That's a good message to leave!

In the first example, by putting forth the assumption—one that we knew was incorrect—that a particular company was easy to work with, we learned that the last book packager with whom this publisher worked tried to win extra payment for developing a book project's index, when the publisher was under the impression that this service was included in the initial contract. Do you think that this unpleasant experience should affect the proposal you develop with this publisher for your next project? Sure it should. In the proposal you eventually work up, you should prominently highlight the fact that the charge includes complete index preparation, executed to the publisher's specifications!

Let's look at the second example, the one in which the prospect fully informed us that sales training simply didn't work for his firm. This interview reflects any number of discussions I've had with people who've hooked up with poor training outfits in the past. In many cases, rather than finding fault with the company they work with, they conclude that theirs is a specialized line of business, one that really can't benefit from sales training.

Now, when people in my company encounter someone who has this opinion of sales training, do we take pity on his ignorance and inform him of the inaccuracy of his position? Do we charge into prosecutor mode and ask him to supply concrete evidence to us that his industry is somehow different from the many others we've worked with—evidence we strongly suspect does not exist? Do we pull out our snazzy color brochure, filled to the brim with testimonials, and read them, word-for-word, just in case he's forgotten how to do that himself? No. We don't do any of these things, because all of them will tend to polarize the emerging interpersonal relationship.

In this second dialogue, notice that we pose a question that allows the prospect to indulge his instinct to set us straight. We made a bit of a guess, and we gambled that the unknown competitor was a local outfit that hadn't yet established itself. Then we asked the prospect whether the training firm was located out of state, with the implication that we believed that it was. This allowed the prospect to correct this—and, in the process, to pass along the critical fact that the "competitor" is in fact a small, and apparently ineffective, firm operated by the CEO's brother-in-law! That's good to know when it comes time to decide how heavily to emphasize our record of experience, follow-through, and orientation toward results later in the process, wouldn't you agree?

How about the third example? We had a suspicion that one of the chief reasons our prospect went with a rival widget company was that it offered liberal credit terms. Instead of asking the prospect to confirm our suspicion, however, we phrased the question in such a way that he got to correct our "misimpression" about how "a lot of companies" set up terms with firms like his. Because this technique was not confrontational—because it allowed the prospect to retain control of the conversation—we got a reward in the form of two critical pieces of information about the target company. We learned that the initial choice to go with Johnell was made in the heat of the moment, with the deadline looming, and that Johnell's credit terms played a key role in winning the sale for them. When it comes time to develop a full proposal, we can try not only to match the terms our competitor offered, but also to raise issues that could have been lost in the shuffle the first time around: quality, say, or long-term service arrangements for the widgets we provide. The specific issues will have to be hashed out with the prospect, of course. And you can bet that framed questions, like the three we've just seen in action, will have a lot to do with the information we gather.

Frame Power!

Framing can be adapted to virtually any type of information gap you need to fill. You can use this approach, for example, when you want to learn about who else is bidding on the order you're hoping to land for your company. Instead of asking that question directly ("Who is my competition for this order?"), you simply propose an option that you have good reason to expect the prospect will correct.

You: So are you working with Plattsburgh Services on quotes for this job? *[Present-oriented variation on Question Number Five: Who Are You Doing It With?]*

Prospect: Plattsburgh? No, no, they're way too small for a job like this. We've worked up quotes from a few people: Eve Media, Maclen Productions, Business to Business. Those are the people you'll be bidding against.

It Works!

This technique of posing a framed question, one the prospect can feel comfortable correcting, has a distinct advantage over most of the other types of questions you'll see examined in sales programs: It really, truly gets people to tell you what's happened before, what's on their mind at the moment, or what they're planning to do in the future.

Just for the sake of thoroughness, let me take a few moments to review the other popular (but not, alas, always effective) types of sales questions trainers may have recommended that you use during your early encounters with the prospect.

General questions are basically the same structure as the getting-to-know-you questions we discussed at the beginning of this chapter. They don't ask for much information, and they usually don't get much. Typical questions in this category sound like: "So how are things?" Or: "Things still working out okay with the system?" Or: "How'd you like the new office?" General questions are typically meant to be answered with phrases like "fine," or "okay," and there's a subtle or perhaps not-so-subtle social pressure for your prospect to answer in this way.

The specific questions are pointed. They don't assume a predetermined answer; they leave the door open for the prospect to give the best response he or she can. The danger with these questions is that they put the prospect on the spot. People aren't great sources of information when they feel threatened. The response you get to a specific question may or may not be accurate, and it may or may not be meaningful. Typical questions from this category sound like this: "Are you the person who handles the decision in this area?" Or: "If we do X, will your organization do Y?" Or: "And when will the president of the firm be making his decision?" Specific questions usually seem unthreatening enough to the person phrasing them—they are, after all, simply straightforward requests for information—but they often carry an unintended emotional charge. These are the kinds of questions superiors ask their subordinates. The temptation to bluff or give information that is completely inaccurate is often very strong for prospects who are asked specific questions. Why shouldn't they mislead you? You're not their boss, but you're acting as though you are.

Leading questions are questions that try to force the prospect into giving a certain predetermined response. This type of question takes great skill to use correctly. Some experienced salespeople manage to use leading questions to highlight problems and determine whether a prospect is likely to buy. Most of the salespeople who engage in leading questions are not highly skilled, however, so the technique is almost universally loathed by the people on the receiving end. Typical questions from this category sound like this: "Are you interested in making a million dollars?" Or: "Do you care about your family's financial security?" Or: "Do you care about the level of quality your customers perceive?" When they backfire, which they usually do, leading questions are usually followed by even more irritating specific questions: "Why *aren't* you interested in making a million dollars?"

The framing technique works consistently, and it works better than any of these approaches—when it's applied correctly. As it turns out, the only sure way to mess up the framing technique is to use it in reverse, to try to get the prospect to "correct" you by making some admission you're bound and determined to yank out, no matter what. In such a case, even though the question is structured as a framing question, it really has more in common with a leading question. If you tried to frame questions in this way (by saying, for instance, "After talking to a few of your customers, I was under the impression that your organization wasn't all that interested in improving quality."), you may rest assured that the framing technique will fail spectacularly. You'll come off as arrogant, conceited, and overbearing. And you certainly won't close the sale.

Similar misfires can be expected if you are so uncomfortable with the very notion of admitting that you're wrong that the prospect can sense your anguish when you concede even a minor point. The framed question must arise from a certain humility—humility with poise, to be sure, but humility nonetheless.

There's a price to be paid for getting important sales information from our prospects. We have to check our egos at the door. And that means we have to be willing to make "mistakes" that will result in our being pointed in the right direction by the prospect. It means we have to assume that the prospect's problem is somehow, in some yet-to-be-uncovered way, different from that of the last person with whom we spoke. It means we can't be intimidated by the idea of being corrected or fearful of posing a question because we think it may expose a gap in our knowledge base. The whole point is to expose as many gaps as possible in our knowledge and then get the prospect to help us fill them.

If we already knew the answers about his prospect's situation, we wouldn't have to listen. But we don't know all the answers, so we do have to listen. In short, we have to give up the instinct that we're always right. And we have to demonstrate that we're willing to be righted.

We're not *Jeopardy* contestants, rewarded for every correct response that happens to be phrased in the form of a question. We're not taking time out of the prospect's busy day in order to show how smart we are. We are facilitators, professional connectors of problems to solutions. Just as a consultant or a doctor or an interior specialist must gather as much information as possible about the situation at hand before formulating a plan of action, we must do the same.

A Dream Come True?

This method of eliciting information is often a tricky undertaking, because there are times in the sales rep's day-to-day work when the prospect appears simply to volunteer all the necessary information. However, those volunteering episodes can be deceptive encounters. If you simply nod and point the person toward one of your solutions, you'll probably get a sale. But you won't build a partnership. Those instances of sublime prospect cooperation, those times when it seems we can do no wrong—when it seems, in fact, that we don't have to do anything in order to close the sale—all those dream-come-true exchanges are almost always traps.

You read that right. Even though you get the sale, those kinds of interactions with prospects typically represent short-term alliances at best. In the long term, these situations are traps in which you are basically invited to warm up the prospect for an eventual alliance with one of your competitors. If you consistently fall for the trap, you won't dig into the prospect's history, as the three framed questioning dialogues we saw did, and you'll probably perform, over time, at the bronze medal level. If, every once in a while, you work up the courage to ask the kinds of framed questions we've just seen when a sale "falls into your lap," you'll sometimes get the key information you need, and you'll likely end up performing at a silver medal level over time. To perform at the gold medal level, however, you must commit to asking the right questions in the right manner, all the time.

You have to be willing to ask. You have to be willing to let the prospect take the lead in responding. And you have to be willing to be corrected.

Beware of the Ritual Responses!

Let me make one more important general point on questioning before we proceed to the next chapter. Some of the dominant patterns in American language and culture in general, and in American business language and culture in particular, make our questioning work harder. As a brief description of initial pleasantries that appeared earlier in this chapter reflects, we live in a country in which questions like "How are you?" and "How's business?" are typically seen as ritualistic conversation-openers. As a general rule, they're not seen as honest-to-goodness requests for information.

When was the last time you picked up the phone and responded to someone's "How are you?" query by actually telling them, in detail, about your current emotional state? Foreigners who conduct business with our companies often complain that Americans are insincere and that we "ask how people are but don't want to hear the answer."

For most of us—particularly men—there is a tendency to shut down when we hear, or phrase, questions at the outset of an exchange with a stranger. It's very easy for people to go into "default mode" and assume that the first few questions of any meeting are basically innocuous, no matter how they're structured. This means that it is incumbent on you to deliver your first question—the one at the end of your company biography, the one I preface with the phrase "I'm just curious"—very carefully indeed. You must deliver this question with the utmost sincerity, and you must make it clear that you are asking because you are interested in hearing the prospect's response. You don't want to have to answer your way out of an exchange like this:

You: . . . which has just been released to bookstores. Mr. Jones, before I go any further, I'm just curious. Have you ever met with a book packager before? *[Past-oriented variation on Question Number Five: Who Are You Doing It With?]*

Prospect: Oh, we met with a lot of people, yeah, in all different categories, all different levels. Lots of different people, authors, agents, you name it. Hey, can I get you a cup of coffee?

If you follow the advice I offered a little earlier in this chapter and actually open up your notepad and be prepared to take notes on this initial question, you will virtually eliminate the possibility of your prospect's shutting down on you in this way.

Chapter Seven

The Past—By Means of the Future

This is the chapter in which you'll find advice on how to explore the history of your prospect's company—which is the essential first stage in assembling a comprehensive portfolio of information about the organization. But the first order of business in developing that information is one you might not expect.

It's a paradox, all right. Before you can talk about the company's past, you must ask your prospect briefly about the target organization's future plans.

Why? Because there's absolutely no point in wasting your time (or the prospect's, for that matter) if your prospecting work has pointed you toward the right organization but the wrong person. If you haven't hooked up with the right person, you need to know that. And by a "right person," I mean either the official decision maker who can say "yes" to what you have to offer or the appropriately placed insider who is in a position to lobby that official decision maker on your behalf. Both of these people, by definition, have some idea of what the organization's future plans are in the area of your product or services. That's why the early part of your inquiry into the organization's past is marked by a question that explores how much your contact knows about future plans.

Of course, you've already asked your prospect something about the past. In the last chapter, we saw how you interrupted your own company's biographical statement with a question about the target company's past meetings with competitors or past use of products or services that parallel yours. (By the way, if it seems appropriate, you can point that question toward whether the target organization ever considered using your product or service in the first place.)

The initial question forms a natural—and, I would argue, indispensable—bridge to a question about the future.

If your prospect seems to display a general ignorance about what's happened in the past with regard to the use of your product or service, there's a pretty good chance that he or she is not the person you should be talking to. Or, at any rate, not the only person you should be talking to. If your prospect has little or no idea what the plans are for incorporating (or not incorporating!) your product or service in the future, guess what? There's no doubt. You need to find a way to hook up with someone else in the organization. There's no point asking this person anything about the company's past. All you're going to get in response is a lot of silence—or, worse yet, inaccurate information.

Your game with the second honest-to-goodness question of the session, then, is to find out how much your prospect knows about the future plans of the organization in the area under discussion. If the person you're after gives you a meaningful, informed response, of course, you're going to take it all down on your notepad. In essence, you're going to ask exactly what Mark did when he started his interviewing phase with the three exhausted executives in the room full of charts and graphs. (To be sure, Mark already had a good idea who he was dealing with, but his use of a future-oriented question certainly didn't hurt his presentation!)

Here are some examples of what the second question would sound like:

You: Tell me—what's the main thing you're hoping to make happen next quarter with the widget project we talked about on the phone? *[Future-oriented variation on Question Number One: What Do You Do?]*
Or:
You: Here's something I'm wondering. What kinds of relationships are you hoping to develop in the future with regard to freelance manuscript development services or book packaging providers? *[Future-oriented variation on Question Number One: What Do You Do?]*

Or:

You: What are your plans for sales training for the next year or two? *[Future-oriented variation on Question Number One: What Do You Do?]*

Or:

You: What areas do you anticipate trying to focus on with your project acquisition next year? *[Future-oriented variation on Question Number One: What Do You Do?]*

Or:

You: Can I ask you something? What are you trying to get accomplished in this area? *[Future-oriented variation on Question Number One: What Do You Do?]*

The last one is one of my favorites, by the way. It's informal, doesn't presume a high degree of technical knowledge (important, since many top decision makers don't possess a great deal of technical knowledge), and it's pretty close to unerringly accurate at flushing out people who aren't in the loop. People who can't help you get closer to a sale simply don't know what to do with the question, and any attempt they make to fake their way through it is usually immediately obvious.

If the person you're talking to seems to have some idea what's going on with regard to your product or service in the future . . . or appears to have a strong sense of what's happened in the past . . . or gives you the general impression of being able to influence matters in one direction or another, even without saying so directly . . . then you should proceed with the interview as outlined in the rest of this chapter.

If, on the other hand, the person you're talking to gives every indication of being a tangential player, as evidenced in the exchange like this . . .

You: So, Mr. Jones, let me ask you this: Is the company planning to stay with a work force that's roughly the same size over the next twenty-four months?

Or:

Does your organization anticipate doing any on-site training during the next fiscal year?

Or:

How many new widget programs is your work group planning to be involved with next quarter? *[Future-oriented variation on Question Number One: What Do You Do?]*

Prospect: Gee, I really couldn't tell you.
Or:
You know what? That's a good question!
Or:
Is that really important?

. . . then you need to say something like this:

You: Hmm. Well, this is kind of important, and let me tell you why. We've found a lot of clients have learned that they were tied to a program that had them paying more than they had to for the service (Or: losing customers; Or: missing revenue opportunities) because we weren't able to work with them to forecast what they were going to do in this area. So it really can make a big difference for your organization. Do you know who we could talk to who could point us toward your company's plans in this area?

In other words, you're going to work with your current contact to help resolve a pressing business problem, and you're offering that person the opportunity to help present the solution to the problem. You're not going to abandon your current contact just because you have concluded that he or she seems unlikely to be in the loop on purchase decisions; instead, you're going to try to turn him or her into a business ally as you work your way through the organization. You're going to make an unspoken offer to turn your current contact into a hero by letting him or her be the one who can bring your solution to the attention of the people who make decisions in your area.

Why Not Just Ask?

You may be wondering: Why can't I just ask whether the person I'm talking to is the decision maker? That certainly seems as though it would be the most straightforward approach, doesn't it? After all, it's not as though you're discussing state secrets here. Either the person you're talking to handles decisions in this area, or the person you're talking to doesn't.

There's a problem, though. During the early parts of the sales cycle, people don't mind in the least lying to you on this point.

I'm sure it's all very innocent. I'm sure that over the years prospects have assembled the whole collection of great excuses for lying to salespeople when it comes to answering this question. But it is an inescapable fact of sales life that prospects do lie when asked about their status as the decision maker. My own experience leads me to believe that roughly half of all prospects asked this question will make an inaccurate, misleading, or deceptive response. This means every other time you ask the question, you're getting bad information. You might as well toss a coin.

If you stop and think about it, this state of affairs actually makes sense—from a certain angle. Most of us like to impress other people, and few of us, all things being equal, are going to de-emphasize our importance to the organization we work for. Therefore, people who aren't involved in a certain business decision have an interest in leading you to believe that they are involved in that decision.

On the other hand, people like to be able to make important business decisions—whether on their own or with others in the organization—in a secluded, distraction-free environment. For better or for worse, thanks to the efforts of the many find-the-need salespeople out there, many businesspeople today have come to the understandable and probably accurate conclusion that most salespeople are distractions. They assume, at first, that you're like all the rest of the salespeople they've spoken to. So, instead of trying to convince you they really are in the loop, some people have an interest in leading you to believe that they aren't involved in making the decision.

Here's another way to look at it. Many prospects think to themselves, "Hey, you may or may not be working with us, so who cares whether I tell you the truth now?"

In the final analysis, the underlying reasons for this information gap aren't as important as our acceptance of the fact that the gap exists. If you're honest with yourself, you'll probably have to admit that your own experience has shown that simply asking the prospect "Are you the decision maker in this area?" is a colossal waste of time, and a great way to find yourself chasing down blind alleys.

Determining whether the prospect knows about future plans affecting your product or service, on the other hand, is an extremely reliable indicator of whether the prospect is involved, at some level, with the decisions that will affect you. So use your second question of the session as I've suggested here. Together with the answer to the first question about a company's history, the two answers you receive will tell you a lot about who you're dealing with and where they're situated in the network of authority that hands down the "buy/don't buy" judgments.

The way your contact responds to those two questions is usually enough to give you a sense of where to go next. Usually—but not always. If the pair of questions I've outlined here doesn't do the trick, and you still feel uncertain about exactly who you're talking to, there is one more avenue open to you. It must, however, be undertaken with great attention and care.

The Last Resort

The "last-resort" query we're about to look at is basically a variation on the most advanced of the six sales questions, Question Number Six. This is a dangerous question and one that, if mishandled, can scuttle the sale for you! So please be sure to deliver it exactly as I outline it.

The key to getting away with this question, which aims directly at finding out who in the organization is involved with making the purchase decision, is not making eye contact during the second half of the question. For some reason, looking the person directly in the eye when you pose this question is almost always perceived as a challenge. So instead of looking the prospect in the eye for the whole question, you're going to look down at your notepad halfway through the sentence and simply await the information the prospect's about to pass on to you. This is an extremely important step—if you ask this Group Six question at this stage, early in the interviewing phase, you must follow this advice if you hope to keep the sales cycle moving forward.

Here's what the question looks like:

You (while looking at the prospect): Mr. Jones, let me ask you this. Who in . . . *(Look down to your notepad and hold your pen in your hand as though you're awaiting instructions)* . . . the organization would be involved in making the decision to work with us on a project like this? *[Future-oriented variation on Question Number Six: How Can We Help You Do It Better?]*

Note that this question does not ask the prospect directly whether he or she is involved in the decision making process. Nor does it attempt to close the sale. It simply requests information and then sits on a nice, fat silence, which is what you should expect to hear when you pose it. No matter how long that silence lasts, keep staring at your pad and wait for the prospect to respond. When he or she does, write down what you hear and proceed accordingly. If you conclude that you do in fact need to reach someone else in the organization, return to the ally-building technique that we just outlined, and try to get your prospect to steer you in the right direction.

Once again: In moving forward to the variation on Question Number Six at this stage of the relationship, you must take great care not to intimidate the prospect, polarize the relationship, or offer any excuse to pass along any faulty information. Break off eye contact as I suggested, and keep your focus on your notepad until you hear the information you need.

Let me be clear, too, on this point: Your aim here is not to march lockstep through the organization until you find yourself sitting across the table from the one, the only Big Kahuna, the person who carries sole and exclusive responsibility for deciding whether to buy from you. Reaching that person is nice when it happens, but you can't make obtaining a face-to-face meeting with that individual your objective at this stage. There are a number of reasons for this, the most important of which is that there may not be such a person in the first place.

At many organizations (mine, for instance), the so-called "decision making authority" on key purchase decisions is diffused among a number of people. There may be one person (or one committee) in charge of researching issues and developing a recommendation and another person who will almost certainly approve that recommendation but who will nevertheless review it closely before a purchase order is issued. Such ad-hoc arrangements are the way the real business world operates, and these arrangements often don't reflect formal titles or organizational outlines.

So don't get misled by titles or flowcharts. For one thing, titles can be extremely deceptive; a contact can have the most impressive title in the world, but have literally no knowledge on the area that title points toward. Titles and hierarchical arrangements aren't the point. Your objective is not to track down the person who can say "yes"—although you should certainly take the opportunity to meet with that person if you find him or her! In most cases, however, your aim is simply to hook up with an insider, someone who knows exactly what the decision process is going to be and who is likely to be able to work on your behalf as it goes forward.

Small Talk That Isn't Small Talk

Let's assume that you use the techniques above effectively and that you've found your way to the right person. Your aim now is to find out as much as you can about the company's history as it affects your product or service—right?

Well . . . it can be. I believe, however, that it's usually just as important to find out about your individual prospect's past. After all, when it comes right down to it, you're not really selling to a company at all. You're selling to another person, a person with a career to think about and a daily series of problems to address, just like you. Depending on the situation, you may decide, once you've satisfied yourself that you're dealing with the right person, to start asking a few questions about the person sitting across the desk from you.

Now, you know and I know that sales calls don't follow a predetermined script. Sometimes, the second you walk in the door, you have a pretty good idea what position the prospect occupies in the organization. And sometimes you don't. When you feel confident enough about the nature and scope of your prospect's job to alter the basic pattern a little bit—and that may happen as a result of information you develop during your cold call, or information you received from the third party, or something you read in a newspaper or trade magazine—you may decide that the initial "small talk" phase of your visit presents you with a perfect opportunity to find out a little more about your prospect's mindset, typical approach to dealing with problems, and career aspirations.

There are a series of "small talk" questions you can ask during the initial greeting-and-pleasantry stage that will help you do just that. I should point out that my own preference is to use these questions only when I'm relatively certain that I'm dealing with someone who is in a position to help me move the sales cycle forward. The reason? Well, people love to talk about themselves, and they love to do so at length. Issuing an invitation to hold forth on one's history, current projects, and future plans often results in some long speeches. When those long speeches come from someone with whom I'm hoping to build a long-term business alliance, I'm happy to take it all in. If I don't know whether I'm talking to the person who schedules sales training or the person who sorts the mail in the morning, I tend to be a little more conservative about the way I spend my time, since it's the single most important asset at my disposal. That's my decision; you may come down differently on this issue.

In any event, whether you decide to do so, you can use the initial meet-and-greet phase of your meeting to get your prospect to open up about personal—rather than organizational—aims, predispositions, and past experiences. The beauty of doing so is that the questions you'll use do just as good a job of managing the social niceties, so essential to a first-time business meeting, as anything you can say about the weather, the prospect's office, or an upcoming holiday weekend. Of course, you can also introduce these questions at later points in the interviewing phase, but my experience has been that, when delivered briefly and with full attention during the small talk phase, these kinds of questions can help you develop a real, lasting rapport with the decision maker that makes all the subsequent work a great deal easier. Nevertheless, I know of a good many salespeople who use these prospect-oriented questions as backups; they appeal to this line of questioning when they feel their main line of questioning isn't going as well as it should. That's certainly a workable strategy, too.

Here are examples that will demonstrate what these "small-talk-that-isn't-small-talk" questions can sound like.

Example #1

You: This is a great office. How long have you had this job? *[Personalized, past-oriented variation on Question Number Three: When and Where Do You Do It?]*

Prospect: Oh, gee, let's see—it must be six years now.

You: Really? How did you get it? *[Personalized, past-oriented variation on Question Number Two: How Do You Do It?]*

Prospect: Well, it was sort of an odd combination of coincidences. An old friend of mine I used to work with got a better job here, and mentioned to the boss that I was closing down my consulting firm. . . .

Example #2

You: I'm just curious—how long have you been with the company? *[Personalized, past-oriented variation on Question Number Three: When and Where Do You Do It?]*

Prospect: Well, I think it's four years now.

You: No kidding. How did you get hired? *[Personalized, past-oriented variation on Question Number Two: How Do You Do It?]*

Prospect: Tell you the truth, it was a temp assignment, but they liked what I did during crunch time so much that they ask me if I'd consider coming on full-time. The first job I held was as accounting clerk, but that only lasted about six months; after that I was moved up to. . . .

Example #3

You: Boy, this is a really exciting company. How did you get started here? *[Personalized, past-oriented variation on Question Number Two: How Do You Do It?]*

Prospect: I was here when they started the place up.

You: Wow!

Prospect: Yeah, I was one of the people Mike called when he wanted to get things going. We didn't really have much in the way of job titles back then; I guess you could have called me the sales manager. All that meant back then was I was the one who'd hire the salespeople and talked to them every day, but a lot of the time it also meant I got to pick up the phone and dial the numbers when it came to reaching new customers. . . .

These are all, of course, questions that point toward the prospect's past, questions that encourage the person to fill in the points as he or she sees fit. Asked with sincerity, the questions serve as tangible proof that you're interested in your conversational partner. Delivered correctly with genuine feeling, these questions can be extremely flattering. They can also be remarkably effective at getting people to open up to you. They may result in some extended monologues—and, not infrequently, unsolicited lectures on career enhancement, corporate strategy, and industry trends. Those lectures, which can often fall into the "long-winded" category, are the reason I try to reserve this type of question for people I'm already fairly certain will be somehow involved in the sales cycle. They're the people I want to spend most of my time finding out about.

The answers you receive to this type of question will also tell you a good deal about the prospect's way of approaching problems, level of education, and degree of experience in dealing with vendors other than a main supplier. Listen not only for the hard facts, but also for the direction from which the prospect approaches key issues. If your contact remarks that he got his job as a result of his ability to "put out fires," and goes on to note that he spends most of his time handling issues of "crisis resolution," there's a good chance that to a large extent he views his job as a series of opportunities to save the day for the company . . . typically by addressing problems someone else missed early on. As you work together to develop your proposal, you'll probably want to formulate your solutions in a way that emphasizes dramatic settlements of potentially catastrophic oversights—with that credit accruing to your prospect, of course.

Past-oriented questions, those on the personal level, will also tell you something about the prospect's personal familiarity with your type of product or service. Resist, at all costs, any temptation to display how your knowledge exceeds the prospect's. This is a dangerous maneuver in virtually any situation; in certain cases, it can be downright suicidal.

Let's assume that your initial "small talk" questions point up your prospect's inexperience in dealing with other vendors. This is a common state of affairs, especially when the organization is making the transition from a smaller, entrepreneurially oriented company to a larger company in which decision making is, of necessity, somewhat more decentralized. In such companies, the entrepreneur who started the company has only recently relinquished control of purchase decisions, and he has probably only done so after an extended period in which he tried to run the whole show himself. Often, the entrepreneur will select someone who has been with the company for some time to make purchase decisions in the area in question. Unfortunately, the entrepreneur will likely have remained with a single vendor for so long that the company has no practical knowledge of what else is out on the market. (A similar pattern often occurs in larger companies that pride themselves on "promoting from within," and as a result develop staffs that haven't even thought seriously about switching vendors for the last ten years or so.) In such situations, the new decision maker, wary of making a high-profile mistake, may adopt an extremely cautious, it's-always-worked-this-way-for-us approach—especially if such an approach is in keeping with the founder's line of thinking in your product or service area. When you encounter a situation like this one, beware. Flaunting your superior knowledge and your vast array of past projects in front of the terrified person whose job it is to decide whether to switch vendors may only serve to intimidate them.

These decision makers are usually looking for a vendor who offers a single significant advantage over the existing product or service provider—but strongly resembles the current vendor in other respects!

Finally, past-oriented questions that focus on your prospect's career, even though they don't directly ask the prospect to talk about future plans, will begin to give you some idea of the contact's promises and aspirations. You'll get a sense of how happy your prospect is in the job, the main contribution he or she makes to the organization, and what level of enthusiasm accompanies discussions of the person's work. These can be critically important factors.

I once met with a prospect who had agreed, somewhat reluctantly, to discuss his company's sales training plans. When it came time to head to his office for the meeting, I knew from a little outside research that the man with whom I would be meeting had personally decided all training-related purchasing issues for this firm for some time. As a result, I felt comfortable incorporating small-talk-that-isn't-small-talk questions during the early part of our meeting.

I walked in. I told him it was great to meet him. I complimented the office. I mentioned what the traffic had been like. I smiled. Each of these innocuous conversational "openers" produced the same result from my prospect: a forced smile and a low grunt of agreement. He motioned to a seat and took his own place behind his desk.

After taking a seat, I decided to use the how-did-you-get-started questions sequence right away, in order to try to shed some light on exactly what kind of mindset I was dealing with.

"Gee, Mr. Smith," I began, "I guess you know this is a very highly respected company. You've got a great job. How long have you been with the company?"

"Twenty-seven years," Mr. Smith responded.

"Ah," I responded. And before I could pose the follow-up, Mr. Smith decided he needed to elaborate on the answer. "Twenty-seven years and two months," he went on.

"I see," I said.

"Twenty-seven years, two months, nineteen days, and one hour," Mr. Smith concluded. I thought perhaps he wanted to break the time down into minutes and seconds so I waited. But the fellow just looked at me with a little grin on his face, so I kept going.

"How do you like the job?" I asked.

"Used to love it. Now I can't stand it," he answered. "I'm going to retire soon."

"No kidding," I responded. "When are you planning to retire?"

Mr. Smith's smile got a little broader. "Four months, eleven days, and seven hours from now. Only thing I'm interested in right now is closing the doors and sealing my boxes. Any other questions?"

"No," I answered, "I think we've about covered it. Thanks for taking the time to get together with me today. You have a nice day."

"You're welcome," he said politely. "You too."

There was no way I was going to get any meaningful information, much less the beginnings of a long-term relationship, out of Mr. Smith. His focus was on getting out the door. And that was totally understandable. Talking any further about his sales training needs would have been a complete waste of his time . . . and mine. I shook his hand, left his office, and, outside the building, made a note in my calendar to check back for another appointment with Mr. Smith's successor on the day after the retirement date that was now etched so clearly in my mind.

Four months and twelve days later, I made an appointment—and I eventually closed that sale.

What Else Can You Do with Small Talk?

Many of the salespeople I work with decide to explore not only the prospect's past, but also his current projects and future goals during the initial "small talk" phase of the meeting. I agree with this approach—as long as it isn't pursued mindlessly. You, the salesperson, are usually the best judge of how much emphasis to place on questions directed toward the prospect's, rather than the organization's, viewpoint, and how many of these questions to ask. Because they can be (and often are) asked during the meet-and-greet phase that precedes your description of what your company does, let's look at some examples of questions that ask the prospect to share his present activities and future plans with you. As we do, however, please understand that you are free to incorporate the questioning techniques that follow at the other points of the interviewing phase as well.

Note that in many of the examples that follow, when you ask about the person, you will automatically and quite naturally be asking about the organization, too.

Example #1

You: So it sounds like there's been some major change of focus in the last year around here. How does that affect what you're doing here? I mean, is this job something that's evolving to meet all these new demands, or is it pretty much settled in terms of the outlines of what you do? *[Personalized variation on Question Number One: What Do You Do?]*

Prospect: Well, I met with the VP of finance in February, and we decided to work through some important changes in the job description, based on all the organizational changes that had been happening since the merger. So, yes, I'm in kind of a transitional phase. We're working to get me focused less on the day-to-day number-crunching stuff and more on the ways I can help streamline operations and eliminate some of the duplication you expect to find when two companies turn into one company.

You: But it sounds as though that's not exactly an overnight process.

Prospect: It's certainly isn't. I mean, I have a lot of organizational commitments that I'm in the process of handing off to other people and other departments. And I can't simply stop paying attention to that. People still need to get sales reports, still need to find out how many customer service people are dealing with what product and why. So it's sort of a balancing act right now.

Example #2

You: So what kinds of projects are you personally handling now? *[Personalized variation on Question Number One: What Do You Do?]*

Prospect: Me, I'm basically in charge of all the company seminars and training sessions, and we put together between twelve and fourteen of those a year. This year, we're budgeting to mount fourteen training sessions.

You: Well, that's quite a schedule. How do you usually determine what the topics are going to be? *[Personalized variation on Question Number Four: Why Do You Do It That Way?]* (**Note**: Group Four question can address the means by which a person or individual makes decisions and are often phrased indirectly.)

Prospect: That's something I discuss with the CEO. He and I sit down for a meeting at the beginning of the year and we set up the broad outline of what we want to work on. Then we review that quarterly and make any changes that seem appropriate.

You: So you're pretty much getting this from the horse's mouth.

Prospect: Oh, yes. This is Mr. Stone sitting down with me in a room, the two of us figuring out what we want to work on.

You: Okay. That's good to know. Now, when you set up these seminars, do you typically try to find someone from the outside to work with, or do you develop all the material in-house? *[Variation on Question Number Five: Who Are You Doing It With?]*

Prospect: I set up about 60 to 70 percent of the programs myself. I mean, I personally write the text and set up the manuals, after meeting with the appropriate internal people. And the remainder of the training is something we coordinate with outside vendors.

You: And you conduct the training right here? *[Variation on Question Number Three: When and Where Do You Do It?]*

Prospect: Yes, right here. Both for things we've developed in-house and for programs, we do all the training right on-site, in this facility. That's very important to Mr. Stone. On the in-house material, I usually handle the presentations on my own.

Example #3

You: So where do you hope this job leads you? What do you want to be doing five or six years from now? *[Future-oriented variation on Question Number One: What Do You Do?]*

Prospect: You know, that's an interesting question. I guess I'd have to say I'm hoping I could continue to grow here at the company. I mean, I like the location, the industry is one I feel I've got a real proficiency for, and I've spent most of my career here.

Adapting to a new set of situations could be tricky. So I've always thought about working toward a vice-president position here; something that would continue to make the most of my abilities and still challenge me. But I need to sign some fairly big books, hopefully something in the personal finance area, before I can think about making a move like that.

Example #4

You: So where do you hope this job leads you? What do you want to be doing five or six years from now? *[Future-oriented variation on Question Number One: What Do You Do?]*

Prospect: It's hard to say. To tell the truth, I've been feeling a little stifled here the last year or so. Who knows where things are going to go, you know? I guess you make the best of things you can. Anyway—let's talk business.

You: Okay, sure. Do you mind if I ask—who's involved in making the final decisions with regard to this training budget we'd be working with? *[Variation on Question Number Six: How Can We Help You Do It Better? Warning!* This question must be executed properly. See the earlier notes on the proper use of your notepad. Do not make direct eye contact with the prospect during the main part of the question.]

Prospect: Well, technically, Jane and I handle that, but you should probably be talking to Allison about some of these issues as well.

You may feel a little skeptical that prospects will actually hold forth on such issues as long-term career planning for you. Don't be. The seductive power of full attention is a remarkable advantage in the sales world; every time I watch it in action, I'm amazed that salespeople don't make better use of it.

The kinds of discussions we look at do happen, and quite naturally, when you stick to the six basic categories. When you phrase your questions in a nonthreatening fashion, and then truly listen to the responses your prospective offers, you can get hold of some essential intelligence. In the last exchange, for example, we learned that our prospect is probably a little restless in her current job. She gave us a couple of nod-and-a-wink indications that she may not be long for this particular company. She tactfully changed the subject when it appeared that she might have gone too far. And then, when we followed up on the uneasiness by attempting to confirm, via the I'm-just-staring-at-the-notepad technique, exactly who would be involved in making the decisions, she confidently pointed us toward someone who did have formal authority in our area. Could Allison be in a position to take over some of our prospect's responsibilities in the months to come? Who knows, but we've been pointed in Allison's direction.

These kinds of exchanges, the ones that clue us in on personal intentions that usually remain buried below several layers of business formality, are only possible when we truly pay attention to the prospect and make it clear to him or her that we're interested in becoming an ally. Purposeful, tactful questions, along the lines of the ones we've just seen, are superb tools for doing just that.

More Questions to Ask About the Past

So much for the "small talk" that can carry big implications for your emerging relationship with the prospect. Let's look now at some of the other ways you can formulate questions about the organization's history during the interview phase.

Please bear in mind as we examine these questions that you do not have to pose them all during your first face-to-face meeting with the prospect.

During some meetings, of course, things will be going so well, and you have so much time at your disposal, that you'll be in a position to query the prospect in great detail about what has happened in the past during a single meeting. (You'll also be able to use the material and subsequent chapters to find out all you need to know about what the company's current operations look like, as well as what future plans are in the works.) At other meetings, however, either you or the prospect will want to cut things short for some reason, and you'll agree to get together to follow up at a later point in time. That's perfectly acceptable, of course. It should go without saying that you should always follow the prospect's lead on this score; just make sure that both you and the prospect are in agreement as to what the next step will be.

When you come back for subsequent meetings, however, you must bear in mind that, unless you have all the information you need with regard to the past, the present, and the future, and unless you have elicited specific suggestions from the prospect on what will be going into your formal proposal, you are still in the interviewing phase. Just as Mark was in the interviewing phase when he showed up for his second meeting, the one the president of the company attended. I usually begin second interviews by saying something along the following lines: "So, Ms. Jones, based on our meeting last time, here are my assumptions . . ." I'll then restate the key points from our last meeting; when I reach a point where new information is required, I'll state my final "assumption" as a framed question, which the prospect is likely to correct.

In the extended questioning dialogue that follows, we'll assume that the dialogue has been preceded by the essential "small talk," "company biography," and "initial question" steps outlined earlier in this book. By reviewing the next series of questions, you'll see how you can use "how" and "why" follow-ups to establish important information about your target company's past. Notice, too, the way that they use this transitional phrase: "Let me tell you why I ask that." This allows you to briefly cite some of the solutions you've been able to implement with your own customers. (But note that this story is now an excuse to launch into the presentation phase!)

You: So, in the past, what have you done when you needed color copies? *[Past-oriented variation on Question Number One: What Do You Do?]*

Prospect: Let me think. Usually, we just send 'em out to the local copy center. That little place, you probably passed that on the way up. It's called Paul's Copies. They do the color copies for us.

You: Okay. So, if you don't mind my asking, why have you decided to go that route? *[Past-oriented version on Question Number Four: Why Do You Do It That Way?]*

Prospect: Well, it happened so rarely. I mean, I couldn't give you hard figures, but most of the time it's just one or two copies. And it doesn't seem to me that it really happens that often that someone even needs a color copy in the first place. Of course, I don't work in the graphics department, so they may have another take on it.

You: All right. Now, how much do you think it's been costing you to make some of those color copies? *[Past-oriented variation on Question Number Two: How Do You Do It?]*

Prospect: Oh, I have no idea.

You: Just as an estimate, do you think seventy-five cents to a dollar would be a good guess? *[Past-oriented variation on Question Number Two: How Do You Do It?]*

Prospect: Yeah, that sounds right.

You: But as far as you can tell, you don't really use color copies that much? *[Past-oriented variation on Question Number One: What Do You Do?]*

Prospect: Right.

You: That's interesting, because a lot of the people I'm working with are finding that they're relying more and more on the color copying technology that's out there.

Prospect: Well, as I said, this is my perspective. If you'd like, we can go over and meet with Chris, who handles our production work. He may be able to give you a better idea of what we're doing. Maybe we should take a few moments with him before you go.

You: Okay, That's a good idea; I may take you up on that. Let me just check a couple of things with you here first, though. Let's see. How many copiers have you had installed here up to this point? How many machines have you had put in? *[Past-oriented version on Question Number Two: How Do You Do It?]*

Prospect: We've set up a total of eighteen machines.

You: All right. Now, how did they all get here? Were they all purchased at the same time? *[Framed, past-oriented Variation on Question Number Three: When and Where Do You Do It?]*

Prospect: No, no. Each was purchased separately. See, each department had a specific copier that it wanted, specific functions that it was looking for. So we've got probably four or five different brands in the building. To tell you the truth it's a little bit of a headache when it comes to servicing them.

You: Yeah, I wouldn't be surprised. Have you had a lot of problems with breakdowns, paper jams, things like that? *[Past-oriented variation on Question Number Two: How Do You Do It?]*

Prospect: Well, I imagine it's probably been no more than average, but the real difficulty has come along when someone in, let's say accounting, comes into my office, complaining that the copier's down, and I've had to stop and figure out which of the five vendors we're talking about, whether the machine's under a service contract, things like that. If I had to make a guess, I'd say that the actual maintenance necessary has been about average for machines of this kind, but the administrative work that goes into tracking down who's responsible for what has probably been a little above average. Some days it feels like a lot above average, to be honest. That's one of the reasons I'm meeting with you, why I said I thought we should get together when you called the other day.

You: Okay. Now, can I assume that, since the machines are all from different vendors, that you haven't taken any steps to connect them and to make them work together on some kind of platform? *[Past-oriented variation on Question Number Two: How Do You Do It?]*

Prospect: Oh, no. Wow, that sounds like a nightmare, considering all the grief I go through when one of them breaks down. . . .

You: Well, let me tell you why I ask that. It is actually a lot simpler than I thought it would be at first. A lot of my clients are putting together packages that allow them to link the copiers together, which eliminates downtime, and means you spend less time talking to a repair person. It also means that when you need to talk to a repair person, everything goes through us so you make just one call.

Prospect: Is that right? You have, what, a universal service contract or something?

You: That's right, we cover everything, handle all the legwork. You just call us, and we figure out who needs to come down to take a look at the system. So, as I say, that's a feature a lot of my clients have found can win them back an hour or so of telephone time when there's a problem.

Prospect: That's fascinating. Because the president of the company is always asking me to try to find a way to spend less time running around dealing with copiers.

You: No kidding. Well, that's important, it's good to know that that's a priority for you. All right. Now, in the past, do the departments that make their own decisions about purchasing a new copier authorize the purchase orders on their own? *[Personalized variation on Question Number Four: Why Do You Do It That Way?]* (**Note:** Group

Four questions can address the means by which a person or individual makes decisions and are often phrased indirectly.)

Prospect: No—they go to the president, and he either approves the purchase order or turns it down.

Look what happened near the end of that exchange. It was only at the end that we learned for certain that our prospect is not a formal decision maker with regard to copier purchase. The final question in this sequence was, in essence, the carefully crafted variation of the staring-at-the-notepad gambit for finding out who's involved in the decision making process. In practice, it would be executed in the same way; with our avoiding direct eye contact with the prospect as outlined earlier.

We did learn, however, that our prospect is the person who handles the various crises arising from the five-way maintenance arrangement. So what can we conclude?

Well, we now know that if we want to tear out every copier in the place and replace it with a new one, we're going to have a tough job ahead of us. Not an impossible job, of course, but a pretty tough one. If we want to get our copiers in there instead of the five competing brands that people are currently using, we're going to have to get five department heads to agree to make the change, and we're going to have to line all five of them up in front of the president so he can approve the sale. That's a tall order.

If, on the other hand, we want to implement a system that will allow the company's existing copiers to work more effectively—and, at the same time, allow us the opportunity to take the inside track when it comes to selling the company the next copier it needs when the time to expand comes—then we may be talking to the right person. That's not to say that our prospect is going to make the decision on his own. Odds are he's going to have to make his case in front of the president just like everyone else. But when he does, he's going to be in a position to take advantage of a significant benefit. And that benefit can be seen from any number of angles. That benefit lines up not only with what the company wants (to get our prospect wasting as little time on the copiers as possible and to get him back in front of his other work), but also with what our prospect wants (not to have to spend time trying to figure out which copier is under a service contract, or how to get in touch with the appropriate service person, or what to say to the people who were screaming about breakdowns . . .).

Notice, too, that the feature we thought would be of interest to the prospect—the color copying capability—turned out not to be an important factor. Others in the organization—Chris in graphics, say, or even the president, whom we may end up talking to at some point down the line—may feel differently. But this person, who probably does fit our definition of "Someone Worth Talking To," since he's in a position to move the sale of our linking system along with the president, doesn't think color copiers are of great importance to the organization.

Here are some brief exchanges that focus on the target company's past. Each begins with a very important question. At some stage in the interviewing phase, you must work this question into your interview with the prospect!

Example #1

You: Just out of curiosity, did you ever consider using our company before? *[Past-oriented variation on Question Number Five: Who Are You Doing It With?]*

Prospect: No, we never really did. I mean, we'd heard about you guys, we knew you were doing a lot of training with some of the companies in town, but we always assumed that you're out of our league price-wise. I mean, it wasn't a conscious choice never to talk to you; we just never put you on the list, because we're under some pretty tight budget constraints here. So when you called the other day, I was a little surprised to hear how you'd worked with some of the firms that face the same kind of cash constraints we do.

Example #2

You: Just out of curiosity, did you ever consider working with our packaging firm before? *[Past-oriented variation on Question Number Five: Who Are You Doing It With?]*

Prospect: No, we hadn't. We'd never even heard of you. That's why I agreed to get together so we could talk. To tell you the truth, I was a little surprised to hear about some of the other publishers you'd been working with. I would have thought that you'd shown up on the radar screen here.

Example #3

You: Just out of curiosity, have you ever thought about working with our company? *[Past-oriented variation on Question Number Five: Who Are You Doing It With?]*

Prospect: You know what? We did. We came awfully close to calling you about a prospecting seminar last year, because I'd heard some really great stories from other people in my industry about the kinds of results you have been able to deliver. Before I could do that, we had some budget problems, and everyone was put on a salary freeze until last February, and I didn't have the training budget anymore. So that kind of put things on hold, then I never really thought about it again after the storm passed.

"You Want Me to Ask the Prospect *What*?"

During my seminars, when I tell people they need to incorporate this have-you-ever-thought-about-working-with-us question into their interviewing phase, they usually stare at me dumbfounded, as though I just told them that they had to turn in an innocent relative to the police.

They say things like this:

- You mean I have to ask that—straight out?
- You mean I have to ask them whether they thought about working with us—just like that?
- You mean I have to ask the prospect to tell me whether we've ever been on the short list—to her face? Why?

Because maybe you were on the short list once without knowing it! And wouldn't you like to find out if you were? And even if you weren't, posing this question directly, without any double-talk or backing and filling, will tell you a lot about what the movers and shakers in the target company think about your organization. This question may take a little practice to deliver confidently, but I assure you that it's worth the effort.

Asking this question will also give you yet another important indication of how involved your current contact is in the decision making process at the target company.

So take the plunge. Screw your courage to the sticking post, and ask the question as I outlined it. Don't sugarcoat it, don't hide it inside another question, and don't apologize for asking. Don't bail out at the last minute and start asking the prospect about his favorite type of music and whether he prefers the Beatles to the Rolling Stones. This is not the time for small talk. Just ask the prospect directly whether he or she has considered using your firm before and follow up appropriately.

What's Next?

Where do we go from here?

What are we trying to sell and to whom? In the example we've been following, there are any number of options for us to point our presentation toward—and that copier linking system is certainly one of them—but remember, we cannot make the presentation until we've gotten much more in the way of specific suggestions on how to shape the proposal. Accordingly, we must focus on the specifics of the company's present operations and future plans.

In the chapters that follow, we'll see how you can use the six basic patterns to get the information you need in those two areas as well.

Chapter Eight

The Present

In the previous chapter, we looked at some of the ways you can determine whether you're talking to the right person; we saw how you can effectively initiate the main part of the questioning process with your prospect; and we learned how to focus your questioning on the target organization's past activities. During the next part of the interviewing phase, you're going to focus on the present.

When you target your questions toward the prospect's current application of the product or service you have to offer—or, with some prospects, toward what the target company is currently doing—your questions, to a certain extent, will touch on issues related to what has happened in the past. If the prospect has decided to radically change the current project's objective, you will certainly want to allow him or her to elaborate on what has happened in the past to cause this change. But the intent of your question in this part of the sale is nevertheless to learn as much as you can about what is currently taking place in the target organization.

In this part of your interview, you are interested in what's being done that day, as you sit across the desk from the customer—not on what the target company has experienced in dealing with or selecting other vendors. That's part of the previous level of questioning. Now you're interested in how happy or unhappy the prospect is with what is currently in place—not on what the target company has planned for the next budget cycle. That's part of the *next* level of questioning.

Asking questions about the target company's present use, or present failure to use, a product or service similar to yours gives you the opportunity to isolate exactly where you stand with regard to the competition. Let's assume that you found out, through your earlier questioning variations on Question Number Five, that your target company is using a competitor. How do you find out how much room there is for you to try to win this account over to your side? By phrasing your questions in terms of the present. Here are some examples of what I mean:

Example #1:

You: Now, am I correct in thinking that your company is currently using the Brown Health Plan? *[Variation on Question Number One: What Do You Do?]*

Prospect: That's right.

You: Are you using their Freedom Plan? I know that's a popular plan. *[Variation on Question Number Two: How Do You Do It?]*

Prospect: No, we decided against that one. We looked at it but we decided to go for their 24-Hour-Care plan instead. It is a bit more expensive, but it seemed to meet the needs of our employees a little better than the Freedom Plan did. We had a meeting, laid out both plans for our people, and the 24-Hour-Care plan looked like the one that had the most people supporting it.

Example #2:

You: So—we talked during our last meeting about how you're doing your training through Impact Training.

Prospect: That's right.

You: I'm just curious, do you really like what they're doing for you? *[Variation on Question Number Two: How Do You Do It?]*

Prospect: Well, in general, yes. We're pretty happy with what they do for us.

You: Do you think their prospecting program is the strongest, or does their person-to-person selling seminar work better for you? *[Framed Variation on Question Number Two: How Do You Do It?]*

Prospect: To be honest with you, we had a little problem with that prospecting program of theirs. It was only four hours long, actually more of a subsection of the main program for that day, and we felt it didn't really address all of the issues on making the most of your prospecting time. I specifically remember, actually, that the president of the company was surprised when he saw the outline for the prospecting section. He thought that someone must have misplaced the second page, and it turned out that there was no second page.

Example #3:

You: I noticed you've just started using XYZ Sales Training. I'm just curious: How do you decide to work with a company like that on an ongoing basis? *[Variation on Question Number Four: Why Do You Do It That Way?]* A lot of the companies I talk to that hold your kind of position in the industry tell me that they use Impact Training instead. *[Framed statement following up the question.]*

Prospect: Oh, no. We never seriously considered Impact.

You: Really? Why is that?

Prospect: Well, I know they have their share of snazzy brochures, and they pass around that impressive immediate kit and that uptown client list, but our CEO read their price list and he nearly passed out. The base program they offered, their one-day seminar, was at least fifty percent higher than the figure we had budgeted for a three-day sales training workshop. We may be big, but our CEO isn't about to spend that kind of money on a seminar. So we pretty much decided to take the permanent pass on Impact.

Did you notice how each of those dialogues encouraged the prospect to open up about the specifics of your competition—usually without asking directly for technical information?

When you ask the prospect, "What should I know about your current vendor?" or any awkward variation of that question, you place the person in a difficult situation. You ask them, in essence, to do your work for you—and in the case of the vendor that the prospect is generally happy with, you ask your contact to choose to subvert a functioning business relationship for the benefit of a newcomer. No matter how pleasant your manner, that's something many prospects are going to feel uncomfortable doing. But when you phrase the question so that it targets what the prospect must deal with on an ongoing basis or has dealt with in the past—the plan selected, the program that's most (or least) effective for the organization, the companies the prospect decided not to go with—guess what? You get an accurate picture of what the present situation really looks like! You have a better idea of where you stand.

Take another look at the first sequence above. Note how you can use a little bit of product information to get a great deal of data from the prospect. Knowing the specifics of what your competition has to offer is a big advantage at any point in the sales cycle, but it can pay off particularly impressive dividends during the present-oriented questioning level of the interviewing phase.

If you don't know what kinds of options your potential customers have to choose from today and what the pluses and minuses of your competitor's current offerings are, then find out! The gold medal salesperson is one who is well informed about the broad range of events in his or her industry, and that specifically includes the products and services offered by the competition. Don't wait to find out from the customer about some snazzy new product or innovative plan that your business rivals have put together. Keep an eye on the industry journals. Keep an eye on the ads. Keep an eye on your competition's catalogs and product lines, no matter what it takes. If you do, you'll be in a much better position to discuss how you can better help the prospect do what he or she needs to do!

Now let's look at the second dialogue and that surprisingly frank question at the heart of it: "Do you really like what they're doing for you?" This question, or some variation on it, is an extremely effective way to pin down what's working—and what's not working—in the prospect's current relationship with a competitor. Many of the salespeople I work with shy away from it because it sounds like a question that's likely to reinforce the positive points our competitors have made. Followed up improperly (with a question like, "Really? Why are you happy with them?"), it is likely to reinforce our rivals' strong suit. But followed up properly (with a question like, "Do you think the X is the strongest part of what they have to offer or is it the Y?" where X and Y are aspects we have reason to believe aren't working out well), you get the prospect to lead you directly to where the weak points are. Try it. It really works!

How about that third dialogue? Notice how the prospect has a couple of options for responding to our query about that recently installed vendor. (That sort of question is a welcome relief to those of us who've been subjected to questions designed to elicit one and only one response!) The prospect can answer the literal question posed, the one that asks how the target company currently goes about selecting a vendor like XYZ Sales Training. Alternatively, the prospect can respond to the framed statement regarding Impact Training and can take care up our subtle invitation to correct our "misunderstanding" about that company's suitability to the target company's needs. Either way, we're likely to glean important information about the company's current method of selecting training firms. (As we discussed earlier, we may also learn that the contact hasn't a clue about how a company selects training firms. In that case, we will attempt to help the prospect elevate his or her status in the organization by outlining a pressing competitive issue for him or her to help us bring to someone else's attention.)

The Main Thing to Remember to Ask

If you remember nothing else about the present-oriented level of questioning, remember this: During this part of the interviewing phase, you must, repeat *must*, work in some variation on the following question:

> **You:** So what is it you're trying to accomplish right now? *[Variation on Question Number One: What Do You Do?]*

Let's assume for the sake of argument that you find yourself in some surrealistically hypercompressed sales cycle, in which unspeakable time pressures conspire against you. Let's assume you were forced to jettison all but one question during the interviewing phase. If that's the case, ask what the prospect is trying to accomplish.

You may remember that in the story that began this book, Mark used a variation on this question at the very beginning of his sales cycle to stand out from the competition when everything seemed stacked against him. There is indeed an argument to be made for leading with this question. Personally, I'm more comfortable with the opening sequence we discussed a little earlier, but if you feel that it is in your best interest to customize your opening and to start the getting-down-to-business questioning period with this extremely powerful present-oriented question, give it a try. Whatever you do, incorporate this question at some point in your interview with the prospect. Then follow up the answers the prospect gives you with appropriate follow-ups based on the six-tiered model. Bear in mind that by asking this question, you're giving the prospect free rein to talk about all current problems, whether individual or organizational in nature, as well as those on the horizon. Do not, under any circumstances, interrupt the prospect during the answer(s) to this question sequence.

Wherever you decide to place the what-are-you-trying-to-get-accomplished question, you will nearly always find that it gives you a distinctive advantage with the prospect. Your competition in general and the bronze level salespeople among them in particular will almost certainly never trouble themselves to ask the prospect anything like this. That's good. That's your invitation to stand out from the crowd.

Here's an example of what this potent question and its follow-ups look like in action.

You: Mrs. Jones, let me ask you something. What's the main thing you're trying to accomplish in your publishing program right now? *[Variation on Question Number One: What Do You Do?]*

Prospect: I'm glad you asked that. I had a staff meeting this morning where I was trying to get this point across to some of my own people, and I'm afraid I'm having a little trouble getting them to focus on it. We need to get back to what we do best—impulse-priced books that focus on specific solutions to real-world problems that business people face every day. In the last couple of years, we've gotten completely sidetracked by this whole video spinoff business. It's just not what we do well.

You: You know, from our conversation yesterday on the phone, it sounds like you've got a pretty good idea of what you're aiming for.

Prospect: I sure do. We have to acquire books first and worry about turning them into videos second.

You: So, tell me, how are you going about making this change right now? *[Variation on Question Number Two: How Do You Do It?]*

Prospect: Well, I've just told all my editors to keep an eye out for emerging authors, people who are still unpublished, but who are writing columns or Op-Ed pieces for some of the major publications. And I've signed up a couple of books myself, of course. I signed a business memos book last week, and I'm talking to someone about a career manuscript right now. But I can't handle all the acquisition myself. It's too big of a company for that. We put out sixty new titles every season.

You: Now, are all of your editors in-house here . . .? *[Variation on Question Number Three: When and Where Do You Do It?]*

Prospect: No, we have a couple of division offices. We have one office in Dayton, Ohio, and another in Fresno, California. That's in addition to the Connecticut headquarters. We also have a few people who are telecommuting who have acquisition responsibilities.

You: Is there one editor you're working with more closely than the rest to help you make this change in focus at your house? *[Variation on Question Number Two: How Do You Do It?]*

Prospect: Yes. Her name is Leslie Hamilton; I hired her last year specifically to help us get back to basics. Leslie and I are on precisely the same page when it comes to where we want to point our list and what types of books we want to emphasize. I'm going to be honest with you. I don't have time to look at every proposal that comes in the door. I have a lot of financial and organizational issues to work with—more than I care to, frankly, but the work has to get done. What I'd like to do is get Leslie in here right now and let you two talk things out. If you have book ideas you think might fit into our program, I think she's the person you should talk to.

In setting up the dialogue you just read, I made a point of letting the prospect go on at some length about her objectives. I did that not so much to emphasize the particular challenges fictional Mrs. Jones faces at her fictional publishing company, but more to give you an idea of the startling power of the what-are-you-trying-to-get-accomplished question. People simply love answering it in great detail, and highly placed people in the organization (such as Mrs. Jones) love answering it in great detail even more than others.

Once you pose this question, you should be prepared for an extended answer—typically, one considerably longer than the one I've outlined here. That's good. The more the prospect talks, and the more you write down of what the prospect says, the better you're doing. When Mrs. Jones talks and you take notes, you're finding out exactly how she perceives the problems she and her organization face.

Why do people open up the flood gates when you ask them this question? The answer has to do with the dynamics of the organization—just about any organization, as it happens. Once you ask Mrs. Jones to tell you about one main thing she's trying to get accomplished, you're doing something that few if any people in her company ever dare to do. You're opening a can of worms. If someone within Mrs. Jones's own company asked that question, you know what would happen? Mrs. Jones would answer it! Then policies would have to be changed, contracts would have to be re-evaluated, egos would get bruised, and initiatives that people have invested their careers in would be reconsidered from the ground up. People within the organization often avoid asking the more important decision makers (and the less important decision makers, for that matter) what they want to get accomplished. A question like that leaves doors opened, and most people in the target company are more comfortable when the doors are shut and the decisions are finalized.

Fortunately, you're not in the target organization. So you can pose that question—and turn Mrs. Jones into a powerful business ally—in an instant.

The what-are-you-trying-to-to-get-accomplished question is perhaps the most essential query you'll read about in this book. It's easy to ask. It requires neither incredible courage nor exhaustive research to formulate properly. All it requires is that you ask it intelligently and stand back and write down the answers in your notepad. If you don't ask it and you don't write down the answers, you're doing your own career a grave disservice.

"Why Are You Doing It That Way?"

Another question capable of producing truly formidable torrents of information is this: "Why are you doing things (or: currently planning to do things) the way you just outlined?" It's an excellent follow-up to pose once the prospect finishes expounding on his or her current top priority. Such a question may not always be necessary, because in many cases, such as Mrs. Jones's above, the "why" of the situation as a whole—or at least your prospect's point of view on that "why"—will already have been made crystal clear to you.

In those cases where you haven't learned much about the "why" of things, however, you should follow up with this question. Here's an example of what it could look like:

You: So what are you trying to accomplish right now in terms of your future training? *[Variation on Question One: What Do You Do?]*

Prospect: (Laughs.) You sure you really want to find out? The main thing I'm trying to get accomplished with training right now, Steve, is to figure who the top 40 percent of my salespeople are and point them toward some training slots to get the very most we can out of them. That's the project I've got to focus all my energy on at the moment. I'm in the process of developing a series of objective criteria I can show to top management that will identify who are in those top 40 percent, and it all has to be hard numbers. It can't be based on any of my own personal perceptions, or any warm and fuzzy stuff about who does the best job of representing the company out there. It has to be something I can punch into a spreadsheet, and I have to decide what it is—closing ratio, total commission dollars, total revenue, whatever. I have to have it all set up within thirty days for all 220 salespeople in the organization.

You: Really? Now, why are you doing it that way? *[Variation on Question Number Four: Why Do You Do It That Way?]*

Prospect: Guess. (Enigmatic smile.) It's because I've been handed my marching orders. The VP of marketing has decided that there are some nonperformers here, and I have to say I agree with him. The top 40 percent, we keep and train at full throttle. The bottom 60 percent, we let go.

Now there's an important piece of information to file!

The Committee Problem

At some point in the interview phase—typically in the past-oriented questioning level or the present-oriented question level—many sales-people run aground. They find their sales cycle dashed against an unexpected rock I call the Committee Problem.

In this situation, the person to whom you're speaking does apparently have some idea how decisions that will affect you are likely to be made, and he or she does seem likely, at least in theory, to be able to help move the sales cycle along on your behalf. But when you try to nail down the specifics of the situation, all you hear about is how The Committee Handles All That.

The reply is, in essence, a variation on the I'm-telling-you-I'm-not-really-involved-in-the-purchasing-process-even-though-I-really-am response we discussed a little earlier. The primary difference is that, in this case, your prospect gives you a reason to believe that he or she is part of the decision to buy and/or knows how to influence that process. That means you're probably on the right track. However, any effort on your part to gather facts or to figure out how you should focus the presentation is met with a dodge similar to one of these:

Prospect: That's an important question. It's one we'll probably be addressing in committee.

Or:

Prospect: You've raised an important issue. It's one the group will need to address later on in the process.

Or:

Prospect: That's something we've been working to establish during the meetings on this. If there's time, I'll raise it again this week.

These kinds of responses are relatively easy to accept if you're talking about the minor details of the sale you feel pretty confident about, or if you're in the final stages of negotiating an agreement with a prospect that has made everything short of a full commitment to work with you. All you do is follow the prospect's lead. If the issue is whether to ship the blue units or the red units, and the prospect says he needs to discuss color selection with the CEO at the next scheduled meeting, you wait for the results of the next meeting.

But when the issues are more fundamental—say, whether the prospect has money in the current budget to work with you—it's incumbent on you to dig a little deeper. Here's an example of how you do just that by means of a carefully constructed framed question. (You're trying to find out about the factors the organization typically takes into account before changing vendors of long standing.)

Prospect: Our committee has a pretty detailed list of criteria to check against when it comes to switching vendors; it would take a lot of time to go over here, and you'd be here with me until dawn.

You: Okay. Now, the training you're doing sounds really interesting. I'm just curious about one point, though—and I know you don't have time to review everything with me now, but on one question, I think it's probably worth our talking very briefly about what you're going to do now. Are you working with the people at Impact because you feel that the cold calling program is really effective, or do you place more emphasis on their time management program?

Prospect: Well, really, it isn't either of those. As far as we're concerned—and here I'm speaking just as one member of the group, you understand—but one of the big pluses the Impact program offers, I think, is their ability to work with the salespeople on their closing skills. That was the part of the training program they highlighted for us when we sat down to meet with them, and that was the part that got our CEO the most excited.

Did you see what just happened? The dialogue I've just outlined for you—a dialogue, I assure you, that parallels my own experience and the experiences of a number of salespeople I've trained—showed how a highly placed, tight-lipped, "committee-minded" prospect opened up like a flower. One minute, he was hiding behind a wall of bureaucratic doublespeak worthy of a government scientist working on a top-secret defense project. That exhaustive formal list of criteria set for the review by The Committee was just too long and too involved to discuss in any substantive way; what's more, the poor fellow sounded as though he'd have to kill us for security reasons if he let us in on any of the secrets contained on that list. In the next minute, our prospect was eagerly volunteering the fact that the single most important factor with regard to the current vendor's training program was its emphasis on closing skills.

What made the difference? What turned our trench coat–clad committee member into a fellow professional eager to share his inside information on what the CEO did and didn't like?

If you have to guess about the answers to those questions, please go back to the section of the book where we discuss the basic dynamics of the framed questioning technique! The reason that even tight-lipped, committee-bound prospects open up when we ask them appropriately framed questions is that those questions give them the opportunity to be right, at our expense! Everyone likes to be right. Nobody likes to be wrong. So we're going to give the prospect the opportunity to be right. In so doing, we melt the seemingly impenetrable walls of the committee and start working with the prospect as a person.

Once we give up our own natural instinct to be right and agreed to be righted by the prospect, we usually get all the information we need about what's currently working well and not working so well within the target organization. If we refuse to relinquish that desire to be right, however, the walls of The Committee will stop us in our tracks every time.

What's Next?

In this chapter, we've taken a look at some of the most important questions to ask the prospect about his or her current projects and priorities. In the next chapter, we'll see how to uncover meaningful information about what the future holds—and learn some strategies for turning all the information you've been gathering into a proposal that fits the organization like a glove.

Chapter Nine

The Future

Posing questions about the prospect's future plans and those of the target company is a critically important part of the interviewing phase of your sales cycle. However, it's the part of the questioning routine for which the salespeople I work with have the most difficulty generating any enthusiasm. Some of them try to find a way to skip it entirely.

That's a big mistake. Even if your copious note-taking with regard to past operations and present projects has left you with lots of detailed material, direct from the prospect, material you will have no problem writing your proposal around, you must ask about future plans at some point if you want to reach your full potential in your sales work. As we've seen, asking briefly about future plans is an excellent way to determine whether you're talking to someone who can help you move your sales cycle ahead. Asking in more detail about future plans, once you've hooked up with the right person in the company, is a habit for success cultivated by gold medal salespeople.

Before we look at some of the specific questioning techniques you'll be employing at this point of the interviewing phase, let me take a moment to explain why asking about the future—which may seem a little superfluous at first glance—is absolutely essential.

The First Level of Business Alliance: The Seller

When you first make a sale, your relationship with your customer falls into one of four categories.

As far as the customer is concerned, you may check in at the lowest level, as most salespeople do, and be considered a seller. That's someone roughly analogous to the door-to-door salesperson that shows off vacuum cleaners or cleaning fluids to every homemaker in the neighborhood or to the person who sells kitchen gadgets at the county fair with a fast-paced "pitch" that never seems to end. We may think that our relationship with the customer is significantly different if we don't sell products that seem similar to these. Nevertheless, if there is little or no rapport; if our sales approach is based solely on the idea of "knocking on enough doors"; if we don't make an effort to find out anything of substance about the customer—guess what? We're in the first category, just like the fellow selling the Magic Whiz Potato Peeler.

We call a hundred people and tell all of them how wonderful our pocket pagers are—in exactly the same way. One of them agrees to let us come in and talk about the system. When we make it in for a meeting, we learn that our prospect is in the middle of a crisis period at work and needs to be able to be reached by his office day and night . . . starting right now, today, and ending thirty days from now. We take out a contract. The person we're meeting with signs it. We close the sale, but we know very little about our customer. We've resolved a short-term problem. We're a seller.

The Second Level of Business Alliance: The Supplier

The next level up is the one in which the customer considers us a supplier. We've earned some degree of trust, and we hold a certain amount of responsibility. But we're still quite vulnerable. Perhaps we come across a hospital that needs a large number of pagers because their current system for reaching their doctors is laughably out of date. Perhaps we realize that the fundamental customer base for our pagers isn't the person being paged at all. The doctors, after all, are the last to know when there's a problem with a system, and once someone figures out that the old pagers aren't working well, it's not the doctors who have to deal with the problem. They have patients to take care of. Perhaps we realize that the real customers we are trying to reach are the internal administrative people who have to find a way to make the system work. So we call those people.

We talk to them. We get them to change from the old, out-of-date system to our shiny new system. We solve the problem. We make a significant group of people happier than they were. We show up on the radar screen as someone other than a quick fix. We're a supplier.

The Third Level of Business Alliance: The Vendor

Now suppose a relationship starts getting even stronger. Suppose we're in and out of that hospital on business visits more or less every month, checking up on how things are going with the system. Suppose we start outfitting lots and lots of doctors and hospital staff with their pagers. And suppose we keep the service going well enough and attend to repair and upgrade issues attentively enough to ward off the competitors that try to steal the account away from us. We're offering an attractive price, but that's not the only reason things are looking good. We've delivered solid results over a sustained period of time. The hospital likes the way we're doing things. We win the long-term commitment to handle the hospital's continuing communication and paging needs. We've set up an ongoing relationship, one that features a certain amount of loyalty. If there's a problem with the pagers, we know we won't be cut loose overnight. We have a pretty good idea that we'll be called in to offer suggestions and guidelines on the best way to deal with any problems that have arisen. We're a vendor.

That's pretty good. Having the customer consider you a supplier is a great outcome and it usually only happens after a good deal of hard work. But it's not as good as your relationship with a customer can get. If you find yourself in the vendor mode, you can—and I would argue, must—try to improve the situation still further. You must try to become a partner—a resource.

The Fourth Level of Business Alliance: The Resource

Let's say the hospital plans to expand significantly and is hoping to keep three new facilities in touch with the central location where you're now supplying pagers. Before the hospital administration commits to its final plan, however, the top staff calls you in for a meeting. They want your input on the pluses and minuses of the four-facility plan they're considering. They don't just want you to handle the communications and paging system in the new buildings. That's a given. They want to hear what you think about the important strategic decision they're about to make, a decision that will mean a commitment of hundreds of millions of dollars. They know you are the best person to talk to when it comes to implementing the communications and paging solutions for their staff. They want to see how you feel about this massive new undertaking they're considering before they commit to it.

The only reason they're doing this, of course, is that you've asked them what their future plans are during your visits over the past few years. You haven't been focusing on a single doctor, or a single pager, or even a single order. You've been asking questions that point you toward the hospital's long-term priorities. And you've taken the information and turned it into solutions to their internal communications problems. Because you've taken care to look at the long-term implications of every system you recommended, you've changed the relationship from a simple buyer/seller exchange to a mutually interdependent situation in which the decision makers at the hospital have grown to depend upon you in an important way. You both need each other. And as a result, you are part of the planning process. You're a partner—a resource.

Any Doubt Which Level You Should Aim For?

The fourth stage is the one you have to shoot for. It's the one that survives budget cutbacks, cutthroat competition, and technological jolts—the things most salespeople lose accounts over these days. And the only way to enter the fourth stage later is to ask questions about the future now.

Every Company Has a Plan

Each and every organization you call upon has a plan for dealing with the future—whether that future is defined as what's happening next week, next quarter, next year, or beyond. Sometimes it's a great plan. Sometimes it's a lousy plan. Sometimes it's a 180-degree turn away from the plan that was in place yesterday morning. Sometimes (especially during a crisis) the plan is so short-term as to be almost indistinguishable from a plan for getting through the day. But the future plan does exist—somewhere, somehow—and it affects how your prospect does business. It's aimed at what happens after the current project concludes, and the more you know about it, the better position you'll be in to start working your way toward that partnership status.

Many salespeople are surprised to learn that the target company's plan for the future often doesn't have anything to do with growth, profit, or expansion. These are common objectives among top decision makers in an organization, and the ways the company is likely to go about trying to attain them are usually the most important feature of whatever plan for the future currently exists. But sometimes the key people in the organization are focused on other issues.

For example, the entrepreneur who started the company and who has personally controlled its every move for ten years may now be ready to get out of the game. He may be fixated not on expanding his company's market share or on helping his people work more efficiently, but on finding a door marked "exit!" In such a case, you can talk yourself blue in the face to that entrepreneur or any of his lieutenants about training programs or book projects or widgets or whatever else your heart desires. Unless you address, at some point, that entrepreneur's key objective for the future, you won't be working at peak effectiveness, and there's a very good chance that you'll be wasting your time. No matter what you say or how persuasively you say it, it's quite likely that nothing of substance is going to happen until the man at the top decides what he wants to do next—and appoints a successor.

Your goal is to understand what people are trying to accomplish and help them do it better. In the case I just outlined, you'd be in a great position to do that if you were a consultant who had experience helping companies manage the difficult transition that accompanies a founder's exit. If your focus lay elsewhere, you might want to put the company in question in the "check back in three months" category.

Sometimes the organization's dominant future plan involves successfully managing their merger or sale. Sometimes it involves downsizing. Sometimes it involves resolving the leadership struggle. Any of these situations can result in a roadblock, one you should strive to identify and react to appropriately. If you can't help the prospect attain the goal his or her organization is focused on, you should strongly consider moving on and investing your most precious asset—time—wisely. Trying to convince the prospect to expand his widget acquisitions activities while his company is teetering on the brink of bankruptcy is a fool's gambit.

Ask!

How do you find out what is the overriding objective for the future? Simple. You ask.

One of two things can happen after you do that, and in either case you'll have a good idea of what to do next. If you get the information you need, you write it down. If, on the other hand, you get a shrug of the shoulders, or a response that leads you to believe you're not getting the full picture, or anything remotely resembling the partial picture, then you try to move through the organization with your prospect by your side. You'll remember that we discussed this strategy a little earlier in the book; a refinement of it that involves a group maneuver on your part appears below.

Either your contact can give you the information you need about the future, in which case you record the ensuing remarks carefully and start thinking about how you can develop your proposal around them . . . or your contact can try to stonewall (or plead ignorance, or mount a bluff of some kind—which amount to essentially the same response). Here are two sample dialogues, one for each eventuality. Notice how each includes a set other-people-in-the-industry reference.

Example #1:

You: Mr. Jones, I'm just curious. I know notice that a lot of the other companies in your field are trying to expand into developing CD-ROM and multimedia products. How do you people stand on that? *[Future-oriented variation on Question Number One: What Do You Do?]*

Prospect: It's tempting, but we've decided for right now that it's really not for us. That's a very competitive field, one with some pretty substantial players involved. It may be a priority three or four years down the road, when the technologies consumers like have been determined with a little more clarity. Over the next year or so, we're putting our energies into developing products that operate on standard computer disks. We know that just about everyone's got a computer that can read those, so that's what we're going to stick with for the next one or two years ahead.

Example #2:

You: Listen, I'm just curious. A lot of the companies we've been setting up health care plans for are considering downsizing campaigns. Do you know if that's a factor here? *[Future-oriented variation on Question Number One: What Do You Do?]*

Prospect: Gee, I'm not really sure.

You: Well, you know, it's probably important for us to do a little digging on that point, and I'll tell you why. This could affect the rates we end up quoting you. If there's a plan like that in the works and I can relay that over to my people, we'll probably be able to set up a plan for you with rates that are a good deal lower than they'd otherwise be. So it might be a good idea for us to work that out and see where the company is going, so you'd be in a position to lock in the very best price.

Prospect: Yeah, I see what you mean. There's a problem though: I feel a little funny about setting up a meeting like that. We'd be talking to the senior VP of finance; I'm not sure how eager she'd be about going over this.

You: You know what? There's a senior vice president on our staff who's done a lot of work in this area and is familiar with how downsizing affects the overall ratings of the benefits your group would be receiving. I think that before I make any recommendation as to how we can help you, he should have some kind of input here. How would it be if all four of us got together and discussed what your plans are? *[Variation on Question Number Six: How Can We Help You Do It Better?]*

Prospect: Well—you know what, I've never done anything like that before, but I see your point. Maybe it would make sense for us to try to get together with Sharon. Why don't I try to set something up with her when she comes back tomorrow and then call you later in the week?

The second dialogue, in which we posed a four-way meeting that included our own "higher-up" connecting with a "higher-up" in the target organization, is worth studying closely.

In my experience, when I phrase things in this way by suggesting that a technical expert accompany me on a future visit, about half of the prospects will go along with the idea immediately, and I'll make my way through the organization without incident. Sometimes I'll get a little static from the prospects who think that I'm trying to apply a strong-arm tactic of some kind by proposing this meeting. I usually respond to this with a story that tells about a specific time in the past in which I've brought another person in to discuss things—and then walked away from the sale after determining that there wasn't a good fit.

You: You know, I was reading in **Publishers Weekly** the other day that a lot more publishers are working with packagers these days. Does that fit in with what your company is planning for the next year or two? *[Future-oriented variation on Question Number One: What Do You Do?]*

That's one way to go. Here are some more variations that can be quite effective:

You: You know, I was talking to a lawyer the other day, and she said . . .
Or:
You: You know, I read in **BusinessWeek** recently that . . .
Or even:
You: you know, I was out at the mall the other night, and it seemed to me a lot of the companies in your industry were . . .

All of these can be effective starting points for framed questions that point you toward the company's future plans. Listen to the responses your prospect offers. Write them down in your notepad! Follow up those responses with appropriate questions about the how and why of this situation. Write these answers down in your notepad!

Highlight what you understand about what the target company is presently doing. Then point that understanding toward the organization's future plans by means of a question, with the aim of being corrected.

The Pre-Proposal Question

The answers to all of these future-oriented questions, when combined with the past- and present-oriented questions you have asked previously, will lead you to what I call the pre-proposal question. This question may take many forms, depending on the specifics of your situation and the instructions you receive from the prospect. But no matter what form this question takes, it will begin focusing directly on the issue of what you can do to help the prospect accomplish the objective(s) you've uncovered.

Here are some examples of what the pre-proposal question might look like:

You: You know, Mrs. Jones, I'd like to put some of our people to work on a proposal that would help us get your widget program pointed in the direction you just outlined. Before we make a formal recommendation, though, I want to suggest that we have a very brief meeting with one of our widget design specialists, so he can get a little more information from you and answer any questions you may have about how we can help you hit the output targets you mentioned. Does that sound like a good idea to you? *[Future-oriented variation on Question Number Six: How Can We Help You Do It Better?]*

Or:

You: You know, Mr. Smith, you've given me a lot to work with here today, and I really appreciate your taking the time to go over all this with me. What I'd like to do is take my notes today and work them up to create a rough draft of what we might be able to help you accomplish—not a formal proposal, because I think we still have a couple of questions to resolve, but a rough draft. Could we get together again next week so I could talk about some of the ways we may be able to help you develop your training program? *[Future-oriented variation on Question Number Six: How Can We Help You Do It Better?]*

Or:

You: I've learned a lot today, Miss Brown. What I'd like to do is go back to my office, work up some numbers, and come back here next week to get your input before we assemble a formal proposal. Would that be all right? *[Future-oriented variation on Question Number Six: How Can We Help You Do It Better?]*

In each case, your objective is to set up a meeting at which the prospect will critique the first draft of your proposal. You must make it abundantly clear that the next meeting is not meant for the prospect to review your formal presentation, but to gain specific input on the first draft of that proposal. (See Appendix B for a sample of such a "preliminary proposal" or "outline proposal.")

Even though you'll be using direct, verbatim remarks from the prospect to develop your first draft proposal, you must still review that first draft with the prospect at the pre-proposal meeting. All your assumptions must be checked, all your facts must be reviewed, and all your solutions must be discussed in detail before you make your formal proposal!

At the end of that meeting, at which you must take copious notes and agree to revise according to the prospect's instructions, you will have a very good idea of exactly where you stand with the prospect. If you have followed all of the advice in this book, you will be in an excellent position to finalize a sale when you submit your formal proposal. (For an example of such a proposal, see Appendix C.)

Urgency in the Sales Cycle

As a professional salesperson, you have to be sure that the questions you ask and the next steps you suggest instill a sense of urgency in your prospects. In fact, you have to "train" prospects to understand that if you are to work with them, it must be within the context of a specific timetable.

Some salespeople say: "We can't train the people we sell to! That would be showing disrespect!" The truth is, though, that it is *your* actions and *your* choices that show the other person what you expect from a business relationship. So, at the end of your meeting with your prospect, as you're on the way out the door, suppose you ask this: "Can you tell me something? Just between you and me, where do you see this going? Do you see us working together this quarter?"

If you ask this kind of informal "urgency" question at the right point in your relationship with the other person, you *will* identify the opportunities that exist.

Think of it this way: Your garbage man has you trained. Let's say he comes by once a week, on Monday morning. He has "trained" you to take the garbage out every Sunday night . . . because he *always* picks it up on Monday.

That's his action; that's what he does. He doesn't pick the garbage up on Tuesday or Wednesday; he picks it up on Monday. If the garbage isn't out on Monday morning—he doesn't care; he skips it. He has trained you to respond in a certain way if you want to pursue a relationship with him, and he's done it without showing any disrespect to you.

Make sure the actions you take "train" your prospects to understand that time is crucial in your sales process. When you start to see the sale lingering, move quickly: either win some kind of commitment for action or move on to someone else.

Key Points So Far

Before we move ahead, please take a moment to reinforce some of the most important points we've covered so far:

- Understanding the selling cycle and finding out what the prospect or customer *does* are absolutely essential.
- Practice variations on the six basic selling questions. There are innumerable variations on these questions, but every effective selling question we ask a prospect or a customer can be broken down into one of six categories, each with a specific objective.
- Use the information you've gathered to lay the foundation for presenting and closing. By verifying your information you'll be

much more likely to develop a proposal that makes sense to the prospect. You'll also be more likely to move forward toward a long-term strategic alliance.

- Close the sale by saying, "It makes sense to me—what do you think?"
- Maintain a sense of urgency in the sales cycle.

Chapter Ten

Verification and Proposal Development

If you have followed the program so far and used the questioning strategies we've discussed, then you're well on your way to developing a customized proposal that will outline exactly how you can help your prospect's company obtain its key objectives. However, as I've suggested elsewhere in this book, you can't expect to get to that "right proposal" point without incorporating some kind of verification step in your selling cycle!

Verification is where you make sure that you really do have a bead on the *reason* for action that will motivate *this* prospect, who is different from all the other prospects you've ever spoken to. In fact, verification is the hallmark of a truly effective salesperson. My personal belief is that those salespeople who are most successful are the ones who make a point of *not* delivering a formal recommendation until they're absolutely certain that a proposal is right on target. Case in point: Recently, we got a prospect to *rewrite* his formal request for bids to sales training vendors because we felt sure that the request incorporated some bad assumptions. Instead of simply "following instructions," we were able to interview key people, confirm what was actually happening in the prospect's sales force, and build a program that addressed the real situation. We got the business.

That's verification.

When and How to Verify

For me personally, the verification step typically happens during the second face-to-face meeting, a meeting where I'll show the prospect what I've come up with and say, in essence, "Here are my assumptions, based on what you told me last time—how does it look? Am I right, or did I miss something?"

And make no mistake: that "based on what you told me last time" is extremely important. You must incorporate some variation on that phrase during the verification substep. This part of the verification process might also sound like this:

- "Based on what I heard from the members of your team . . ."
- "Based on what you and I discussed on the phone since we met last . . ."
- "Based on the materials you sent me . . ."
- "Based on what your president said when we met with him . . ."
- "Based on what we found out from your technical team . . ."
- "Based on what you and I saw from the trial program . . ."
- "Based on what we're hearing from your managers . . ."

Once you've said something like this, you should *briefly* describe your assumptions about the situation. Then you must clearly and unambiguously *ask if you are on the right track*.

What you ask at this stage could sound like this:

- "Is that on target?"
- "Have I outlined the situation accurately, do you think, or have I left something out?"
- "Is that about right?"
- "Have I left out anything crucial?"
- "Have I overlooked anything?"
- "Does that seem accurate to you?"
- "Does this all make sense so far, or am I overlooking something important?"

Remember: *It's not verification if you don't give the other person some impossible-to-ignore opportunity to correct you.*

As I said, I usually verify the prospect's information during the second face-to-face meeting. There are a couple of reasons for this. First, my selling cycle typically unfolds over a maximum of three in-person meetings, and the second meeting is often the "midpoint" of the new relationship. The second reason is that by the second meeting I usually have enough rapport built up with the other person to get a little clearer picture of what's going on than I had from the first meeting. This is an important feature of selling that salespeople typically overlook. The *older* your relationship is with the other person, the *better* the information you are likely to get from that person. Yet another reason to be sure you verify what you think you learned during previous discussions!

In *your* selling environment, the best place for verification may occur before or after that second meeting; it could even occur over the telephone.

For salespeople who never meet face-to-face with their prospects, the verification substep might be a fax or e-mail version of the outline (which can be thought of as a preliminary proposal), followed by a phone discussion. Be careful, though. The danger of using a faxed or e-mailed outline is that the prospect might either a) ignore it or b) read it and then never take your call again. Whenever I am transmitting information in some medium other than a face-to-face meeting, I make an effort to set the Next Step before I send the information along, so the prospect and I can review and discuss it together. For instance:

> **You:** Okay, so I'm going to develop a quick overview of what our proposal might look like—but there are a couple of elements I'm going to have to explain as we go through it. Why don't you and I talk by phone on Monday morning at 10:00 so I can walk you through the document?"

Alternatively, inside reps may conduct the verification substep by means of a straightforward verbal summary:

> **You:** Based on what you've told me so far, your aim is to increase your sales by 35 percent this quarter over the same period last year. I'm also hearing that you're interested in learning more about how we

could help you set up an inbound toll-free line to support your direct mail campaigns and your customer service department. Am I on the right track?

I've trained many, many telesales professionals to gather and verify information during a single phone call and then close the sale.

Uncovering Problems

Verification, as we have seen, is a substep of the interviewing or information-gathering step. It's where you try to identify any problems or challenges *before* attempting to close the sale. A successful verification of your information will often lead you to uncover something you didn't know before about what might stand in the way of your doing business with the other person. This new piece of information is likely to be preceded by the words, "Well, you see, the thing is . . ."

Think of verification as the process of getting the other person to say, "The thing is . . ."

The strategy of verifying information allows you to enlist the prospect's help in creating the final proposal, presentation, or plan. Regardless of how long it typically takes you to close a sale, and regardless of what form your plan proposal takes, you must—repeat, MUST—verify your information before making a formal recommendation. Sometimes, if you're dealing with a person with whom you've already got a very strong relationship (a former customer, say) then verifying your information can be as simple as saying, "So . . . has anything changed since you and I spoke last?"

For emerging relationships, though, I recommend that you do what I do: use a written outline—a preliminary proposal—as a reason to get together for a second or subsequent meeting *and* as a tool for eliciting feedback from the prospect. This document is basically a preview of what you think your proposal will do, but in *highly condensed form.* (See Appendix B for an example.) You might begin your discussion of the outline by saying something like this: "Based on what we discussed last time, here are my assumptions . . ."

Then review—*briefly*—what you've come up with. Do exactly what I've laid out in this chapter for you. Conclude by asking something like this: "That's what made sense to me, based on what we discussed last time. Does it make sense to you? Have I left anything out?"

Then *stop talking* and see what the prospect says.

One more point: When presenting a preliminary proposal, don't be afraid to raise the tough issues yourself. In fact, when I'm not happy with the quality of the information I've gathered in a certain area, or when I anticipate some kind of problem from the prospect, I will make a question about that area the *first* thing I ask in the discussion about the outline. For instance: "I'm a little concerned about the price. I still don't know what your budget is, and I really don't know if this price is going to work for you or not. What do you think?" (At this stage, the prospect will have to make some kind of response—and I'll be perfectly positioned to ask, "What kind of pricing *were* you looking for?")

Be Concise

Sometimes people build "outlines" that are twenty or thirty pages long. Please bear in mind that the outline or preliminary proposal is a *concise* (one- or two-page) discussion of your plan—a few sheets of paper that say, in essence, "I am not a proposal." Basically, the outline is a preview of the full proposal—a short summary of the *reason* for working together. It's a document that says, "Based on what we discussed last time, A, B, and C are important to you. Here's one paragraph on how we would deliver A. Here's one paragraph on how we would deliver B. Here's one paragraph on how we would deliver C. Here's what our pricing would look like. Here's our timetable."

It's short, it's sweet, and it's not meant to be the last word. If the prospect reads it, scribbles all over it, changes your wording, and makes you expand and rewrite it—then congratulations are in order. You just won. You successfully used an outline to verify your information.

Don't think that concise means incomplete, though. No matter what length it is, *your outline or preliminary proposal must specify the prospect's objective, all key assumptions, all appropriate dates, your implementation plans, prices or price ranges, and all relevant product/ service details.*

Why Verify?

Some salespeople don't verify because they're afraid of making a mistake in front of the prospect. Here's the problem with that way of working: If you're never corrected by the other person, the odds are that your plan *won't* make sense to him or her!

Think about it: The opposite of "wrong" is "right." You want the prospect to "right" whatever you've gotten "wrong." That means that when the prospect corrects you . . . you win!

Remember: 75 percent of your work in the selling cycle should come *before* you put together a formal presentation. If you verify your information, you'll be sure that you're building the full document around the reason that actually does make sense for this person to do business with you.

One More Tool for Verifying

After I've concluded the main portion of the second meeting, and after I feel confident that I've confirmed the *reason* that the full proposal should be built around (say, improving the team's sales revenues by 15 percent before the end of the next quarter), there's one more question I ask my prospect, just to be sure.

First, I'll be sure to set my Next Step with the person (the time and date we will next speak about our deal). Then I'll "end the meeting." This means I'll start chatting about nonbusiness issues and put on my coat and get ready to go out the door. And finally, once I've "ended the meeting," I'll shake the person's hand, thank the person for taking the time to meet with me, look him or her in the eye, and say, "Ms. Jones, I feel this meeting went really well, and based on what you told me here today, I don't see any reason why we shouldn't be able to finalize this the next time we meet. That's where I am—*is that where you are?*"

The answer to this question will tell me *exactly* where I stand with this prospect!

I have a Golden Selling Rule: Never deliver a presentation you don't think will close!

The corollary to that rule is pretty simple: If the prospect doesn't *know* you're about to try to close the deal, you shouldn't try to close the deal! By making the statement and asking the question above, both you and your prospect will know just how things stand.

The Formal Proposal

If you do exactly what I've suggested here, and follow the steps precisely as I've laid them out, then you'll have a very good idea of what should go into your formal proposal. Not only that, you will have identified any potential obstacles to working with this person *before* you make your formal recommendation.

If you think you are ready to deliver your formal presentation to the prospect, ask yourself the following questions:

1. Am I talking to the right person—the actual decision maker or the person who can get the decision made for me?

2. Have I verified my information?

3. Does my plan/proposal use *word-for-word* feedback based on notes I've taken during discussions with the prospect? Am I sure I am really "speaking this person's language"?

4. Does this person KNOW that I intend to close the sale at the next meeting? If not, why not?

5. Does the plan I am preparing to put forward MAKE SENSE, given what I have learned about what this person is trying to accomplish?

6. Does this person agree with my pricing?

7. Do I know that this person agrees with my timetable? Is there a specific date for implementation/start-up/switchover?

8. Have I prepared parables—success stories—that will help the prospect to visualize what I'm saying?

A single "no" answer to any of these questions means you are not yet ready to ask for a commitment to do business with this prospect.

What's Your Next Step?

Verified information should lead you to a formal proposal—one that *both you and the prospect* expect to lead to a new business relationship.

After explaining (not reading) your formal presentation to the prospect, you'll be in a position to incorporate a variation on Question Number Six. When you do this, you won't be trying to impose anything on the prospect that he or she isn't prepared for. You won't be trying to overcome any obstacles; you will have identified all those well beforehand, and you will have resolved them by addressing them head-on in your formal presentation.

In other words, when it comes to confirming your new business relationship with the prospect, you will simply be acting in accordance with all the work you've done up to this point. You won't really be "finalizing" anything or "closing" anyone—you'll be suggesting specific ways to act on all of the issues you and the prospect have been exploring in the previous three stages. Far from ending anything, you'll be beginning an important new business alliance.

Here are some examples of how your final-phase Group Six Questions might be formulated.

You: Well, Mr. Smith, that's our proposal. Let me be totally honest with you: I think we could really benefit from working together. What do you think? *[Variation on Question Number Six: How Can We Help You Do It Better?]*

Or:

You: Mr. Smith, that's our proposal. I have to tell you, I think your organization would stand to benefit from working with us on this program. How does it look to you? *[Variation on Question Number Six: How Can We Help You Do It Better?]*

Or:

You: Mr. Smith, over the last couple of weeks we've spent a good deal of time developing this together. Looking at it now, I've got to admit that I have a pretty good feeling about this. How do you feel about it? *[Variation on Question Number Six: How Can We Help You Do It Better?]*

Or:

You: Mr. Smith, that's our plan. It really makes sense to me. Does it make sense to you? *[Variation on Question Number Six: How Can We Help You Do It Better?]*

Or:

You: Mr. Smith, that's our plan. I really think we should get started on the sixteenth. Does that make sense to you? *[Variation on Question Number Six: How Can We Help You Do It Better?]*

If the plan *doesn't* make sense to the other person, these questions will reveal exactly *why* it doesn't make sense!

Is There a Problem Here?

If, as you present your proposal, your prospect responds with some objection you've never heard of before or tells you there's no money in the budget, guess what? Something went wrong at the pre-proposal stage! These are issues that should have been addressed earlier, and you have to address them now by asking appropriate questions. You may think you're in the homestretch, but you really haven't yet made it out of the interviewing phase.

If you do encounter resistance at this point in the sale, consider using the following three-step process to keep the discussions moving forward:

1. IDENTIFY the issues. Don't respond instinctively or combatively. Don't offer to drop your prices. Step back from the situation and ask questions like, "What makes you say that?" and "How does this affect your goal of . . .?" Then ask yourself: Do I really understand the problems my prospects typically face? What is this problem, really? (Remember that your prospect's initial assessment of an issue may be masking a deeper challenge.) How is this particular issue affecting this particular prospect, right now? Try to find a way to keep the discussion from becoming too tense, so you can learn what the real issues are. (One of my salespeople has a great way of doing this when it comes to price negotiations. If the prospect says, "We've got a problem on the price," my salesperson says, "Really? Is it too low?" This always gets a laugh—and it depressurizes the situation and makes it a little easier to find out how far apart the two sides really are.)

2. VALIDATE the issues. Figure out what the real-world dimensions of the issue are. Talk the challenge through openly and honestly with your prospect. (For instance: "You're not alone. My experience is that, if people have a problem with our delivery dates, it usually comes up at this point in the discussion. Let's see what we can do.") Don't run away from the problem or pretend it doesn't exist. Offer appropriate additional information and help your prospect reach a logical conclusion.

3. RESOLVE the issues. Doing so may not be as hard as you imagine. Of course, every prospect is unique, and so is every sale. My experience is that accomplished salespeople tend to face the same half-dozen or so "endgame" issues over and over again. You shouldn't try to use a cookie-cutter approach in dealing with the questions and obstacles your prospect raises, but you *should* be ready to "paint a picture" by appealing to appropriate success stories. Be optimistic. Send the message, "We can work this out." Then use your experience to develop a solution.

So much for the obstacles you may face after delivering a formal proposal. It is just as common, though, for sales reps that follow this program closely to hear:

Prospect: It looks pretty good. When do you think we could start?

A Note on Existing Accounts

In this book, we've focused primarily on applying proper questioning and interviewing techniques to the prospects that represent new business for you. That's only natural; getting new business is one of the top priorities of any successful salesperson. One of the distinguishing features of gold medal salespeople is how they understand that they can't rely on current business to see them through forever.

However, I urge you to adapt the six-category questioning model we've been using in your current accounts as well. Take the time to find out (or confirm) the main thing they're trying to accomplish in the organization. Find out how and why they decided to work with you in the first place. Find out exactly how well your solutions are performing. Treat these critical business allies with the same respect, loyalty, and understanding you apply to prospects.

Never stop working toward the goal of turning your current or potential customers into partners. That's the path that will lead you toward that gold medal.

Chapter Eleven

Questions to Ask Yourself

I've shared a lot of myths and misconceptions with you about questions in this book. But I haven't covered the misconception about questions that represents the gravest danger to the careers of most salespeople. It has to do with the kinds of questions we ask *ourselves*. All too often, we salespeople ask questions of ourselves that reinforce the limitations about our own potential that we have convinced ourselves to believe. And we choose *not* to ask questions that reinforce our strengths and our aspirations.

Whenever I run into a salesperson who tells me, "I'm good at X, but I'm terrible at Y, and I always have been," I know I'm talking to a salesperson who doesn't know how to ask himself or herself good questions. We talk ourselves into believing that there's no way we can overcome certain skill gaps, no way we can develop certain abilities, no way we can hit our highest potential as salespeople in all the relevant areas.

Ask yourself questions like:

- "What can I learn from this situation?"
- "How can I improve my skills in this area?"
- "Who else can I talk to?"
- "What has worked for me in the past when I've faced a situation like this?"

- "How can I grow and become stronger by facing up to this challenge?"
- "What do I know today that I didn't know yesterday?"
- "What do I want to learn about tomorrow?"

This kind of commitment to self-improvement is a lifelong process. It is only by committing ourselves to continuous growth in this way that we can overcome the most debilitating sales myth of them all: that there are limits to our own abilities. Good luck!

How Effective a Salesperson Are You?: A Self-Test

Selling successfully requires high performance in fifteen key areas. Take the following brief test to find out how effectively you're selling right now . . . and where there's room for improvement.

How many of the following energy statements can you honestly say are "True"?

1. I understand my own ratios. I know how many dials I must make to get one appointment. I know how many appointments yield a single sale. T / F

2. I know exactly how much time it takes me to hit daily call targets. I commit to a specific time slot for phone prospecting every day. I actually make prospecting calls during that time period nineteen out of every twenty business days. T / F

3. I make a consistent number of prospecting calls each day. I commit to a numerical call target that supports my income goal, and I hit my regular call quota nineteen out of every twenty business days. T / F

4. The number of first appointments I set each week is predictable. I know and hit my target numbers and they support my income goals. T / F

5. It generally takes me no longer than forty minutes to set up a first appointment. I quickly generate commitments for face-to-face meetings because I keep my average call length short. T / F

How many of these efficiency statements can you honestly say are "True"?

6. I understand my closing ratio. I can routinely predict, with accuracy, exactly what I am going to close over the next thirty days. T / F

7. I understand my own timeline and sales cycle. I know the longer a prospect exceeds my average selling cycle, the less likely he is to buy. Thus, I never waste time talking to people in "permanent pending" mode. T / F

8. I am process-oriented. If someone does not schedule a next step, I consider that to be a "no" and move on to someone else. I avoid spending time preparing materials for people who have not made a commitment to moving through the sales process with me. T / F

9. I know how to make my product or service fit in a variety of situations. I can deliver at least ten "success stories" that correspond to different market situations. T / F

10. I spend no more than ninety minutes a day preparing for subsequent appointments. I don't spend all day preparing proposals. T / F

How many of the following value statements can you honestly say are "True"?

11. I understand my firm's pricing points and margins. I know why things are priced as they are. I have no doubts about when (or not) to discount. T / F

12. The pricing I use to develop proposals is, in most cases, realistic and rooted in knowing what makes sense to the prospect. T / F

13. I take a long-term view of the account. I know when it makes sense to set up a plan with management that will lay the foundation for a lengthy relationship between my company and a prospect. T / F

14. I don't have to take every deal. I prospect regularly enough and have enough prospects moving forward that I feel comfortable walking away from a deal. T / F

15. I am comfortable with handling price issues. I know the value my company delivers. I am comfortable discussing that value, and I do not discount impulsively. T / F

Total the number of T (true) answers circled. People who score between 11 and 15 on the questionnaire are likely to be above average performers. That means roughly 50 percent of their formal presentations to qualified decision makers will actually close. Those who score between 6 and 10 on the questionnaire are likely to be midlevel performers. That means roughly 33 percent of their formal presentations to qualified decision makers will actually close. Finally, people who score between 0 and 5 on the questionnaire are likely to be "needs improvement" performers. That means 25 percent or fewer of their formal presentations to qualified decision makers will actually close.

A Sample
Preliminary Proposal

CALIBER PRINTING

Preliminary Proposal for

TREMONT SOFTWARE

Presented by:
Peter Philips
Caliber Printing and Design
pphilips@caliber.com
718-555-0982

Caliber Printing and Design
26-05 Queens Boulevard
Forest Hills, New York 11597
(718) 268-0982

Ms. Erin Steele, Director
Tremont Software
265 East 97th Street
New York, New York 10127

Dear Ms. Steele:

Thank you for meeting with me last week to discuss the opportunity for our companies to develop a relationship. What follows is a preview of the formal proposal we would like to develop for your firm.

Caliber Printing and Design has been providing exceptional printing, production, and design services to a broad range of organizations since 1969. The approach we have designed for Tremont Software will enable you, as you requested, to:

- Turn around your instruction manual faster
- Dramatically upgrade the appearance of your software package

I look forward to working with you on this exciting project.

Sincerely,

Peter Philips

OVERVIEW

Based on our previous discussions, Caliber Printing and Design will address the following project elements for Tremont Software:

Our Program:

1. **Tremont Fast Pak Design:** The experienced graphic arts team at Caliber Printing will work with you and your staff to develop a fresh new design for Tremont's successful product, the Fast Pak. The design will help improve the image of the product, which could help increase sales.

2. **Development of Fast Pak Package:** Once the design has been approved, Caliber will proceed to create samples of your Fast Pak instruction binder, the DVD, as well as the matching box that these items will be sold in. These samples, and the relevant specifications, will be sent to you for approval.

3. **Printing/Assembly:** Upon receipt of PDFs from your team, Caliber will print an initial run of 5,000 pieces of the Fast Pak, and assemble the components, the binder, the paper inside, the DVD and the box, and prepare them for shipment.

4. **Stand-by packages:** We will be on call to print another run of 5,000 copies or more at these rates at any point over the next twelve months, assuming we can receive seventy-two-hour advance notice on your order.

Our Pricing and Implementation Plan:

1. Design work: **$2,000.00**, with changes after approval charged at $75.00 per hour. This assumes our graphic artists can meet with you on October 3, 2005, and the design will be ready for approval by October 9.

2. Development of Binder, DVD, Box Package, and specifications: **$250.00**; materials can be prepared one week after approval of design.

3. Printing run of 5,000 pieces: This includes the Binder, up to 100 pages within, the DVD case and the Box, as a four-color job, and assembly and shrink-wrapping for "market ready" packages 5,000 pcs @ $11.75 each = **$58,750.00**

4. Standby for another run of 5,000 or more units: **No charge**, as long as we have seventy-two-hour notice.

Base price: **$61,000**

Our Web site monitoring service is free, and so is our twenty-four-hour 800 help line.

Timing:
In order to fulfill your launch date of November 28, we strongly recommend beginning the graphic design process on or before **October 3rd**.

Contact:
Peter Philips
Caliber Printing and Design
pphilips@caliber.com
718-555-0982

A Sample Proposal

On the following pages, you'll find a sample proposal, based on the information gathered during a series of face-to-face meetings and verified by means of a single-page "outline" or "preliminary proposal" document.

In other words, the prospect helped to create the final proposal. This should always be your goal.

D.E.I. MANAGEMENT GROUP

SALES TRAINING OUTLINE
FOR SUPERIOR HEALTHCARE

Outsourcing Sales Training for Superior Associates
Throughout the Country

CONTENTS

E-Learning Overview . . .
THE SUPERIOR/D.E.I. PARTNERSHIP

A Comprehensive Sales Training Outline

ROLE OF THE SUPPLIER

D.E.I. Management Group will provide sales training to Superior associates through a variety of methods, and will implement the training as required around the country. D.E.I. will develop pre-workshop activities, the core programs, and reinforcement plans that include on-site visits, conference-call refreshers, and e-learning options. D.E.I. will also provide Superior with the option of certifying Superior trainers to deliver the program themselves; in this event, D.E.I. will ensure that training is delivered according to the highest possible standards.

CRITERIA

The sales training will be based on the following criteria:

1. The **multiphase training** program will be based on the sales training objectives identified by Superior Health Care Services.
2. The **core training** will be conducted by senior D.E.I. instructors. We propose Steve Borromeo, Andrew Norad, or Bob Daltrey. (See trainer biographies below.) Initial training will take place at Superior's Orlando Learning Center.
3. D.E.I. will provide **all written learning materials, manuals, tests, and tools**. D.E.I. can also provide out-of-the-box and customized **e-learning reinforcement programs**. (Visit *www.dei-sales.com* to learn more about our e-learning resources.)
4. D.E.I. will provide **sales exercises for practice** using materials provided by Superior.
5. D.E.I. can execute **follow-through programs based on both on-site visits and conference calls**, and can administer **tests provided by Superior** in order to test applicants' knowledge and skill following the training sessions.

A breakdown of the programs appears on the following page.

OVERVIEW OF PROGRAMS

Note: This is a preliminary assessment. All elements of this overview are subject to further revision from Superior and D.E.I.

Subject	Timing	Target positions	Participants per annum	Length
Introductory Sales Course Covering: • Appointment Making • Getting to "Closed" (Prospect Management) • High Efficiency Selling Skills	Periodically throughout the year	Home Care Specialists	90	3 days
Intermediate Level Sales Course Covering: • Advanced Interviewing Skills • Getting to "Closed" (Prospect Management)	Periodically throughout the year	Account Representatives	50	2–3 days
Advanced Level Sales Course Covering: • Account Penetration Workshop • Getting to "Closed"	Periodically throughout the year	Senior Account Representatives	20	2–3 days
Sales Negotiations Course: • Negotiation Skills Workshop	Periodically throughout the year	Account Representatives	40	1 day
Manager's Workshop covering: • Coaching for Increased Productivity	Periodically throughout the year	Sales Managers	20	2 days
Executive Selling and Strategy (for large accounts, payors, and managed care companies) • Major Account Workshop	Periodically throughout the year	Senior Account Representatives/ Account Representatives	20	2 days

For information on electronic placement and fulfillment of orders, contact Scott Forman (*sforman@dei-sales.com*).

REFERENCES

Mr. John Jones
Chief Marketing Executive
Pennsylvania Healthcare
444 Independence Way
Philadelphia, PA 19011
(215) 555-5555

Mr. Mark Miller
Chief Marketing Executive
California Healthcare
555 Millwood Drive
San Rafael, CA 94901
(415) 555-5555

PRICING BREAKDOWN

We quote a per-person, per-day training fee of $XXX.

The materials-package fee per person will be billed at $XXX.

Reinforcement programs and e-learning fees will be determined through consultation with client.

INVOICING

Here is a sample invoice from D.E.I. Management Group.

Company Name Contact Name Address Attention:				**Invoice**
Invoice Date	Invoice Number	Payment Terms	P.O. #/REF#/ CONTACT	Due
10/11/05	1022021	Net 7 Days	REF# 020912-MSS	

Description	Amount
TRAINING FEE Initial fee (50% of $2,000) for conducting a 1½-Hour Keynote Speech on Nov. 15th in CA, as per agreement	$1,000.00
In the event of nonpayment D.E.I. Management Group shall be entitled to recover from you all monies due and owing, including, but not limited to, interest, charges, and reasonable costs of collection, including attorneys' fees and court cost **MAIL PAYMENT TO:** D.E.I. MANAGEMENT GROUP, INC. 888 Seventh Avenue, 9th Floor New York, NY 10106 FED-ID#13-2976697 GST #R 887262624	TOTAL $1,000.00

KEY PERFORMANCE INDICATORS

D.E.I. has the capability to deploy both **existing and customized e-learning reinforcement tools** for each of the Superior program elements, as described above.

We will work with Superior to identify specific performance criteria and self-test content related to:

- Daily prospecting targets
- Prospect management categorization
- Next Step strategy development
- Phone contact and face-to-face meeting strategy development
- Presentation plans
- Coaching plan development
- Negotiation strategy development

. . . as well as other essential performance indicators, subject to Superior approval.

- **If e-learning programs are utilized, each participant will be required to complete the online certification component associated with any program he or she has completed; a "passing" certificate will be generated for each participant who successfully completes the online performance indicator review section.**

IMPLEMENTATION, ROLL-OUT, AND SUPPORT

D.E.I. proposes the following schedule:

- Mid-May, 2005: Award of contract. Initial meetings between Superior and D.E.I. Creative Services Team.
- June, 2005: D.E.I. Senior Writer Brandon Toropov conducts interviews with selected Home Care Specialists, Account Representatives, Senior Account Representatives, and Sales Managers.
- Early July, 2005: PDF files reflecting customized workbooks to Superior for review.
- Mid-July, 2005: PDF files reflecting customized role-play exercises, tests, and online content to Superior for review.

- After final signoff on above: online content posted on secure site; access instructions forwarded to Superior for content review. PDF files reflecting train-the-trainer materials forwarded to Superior for content review.
- Projected rollout date of initial program: August, 2005.

D.E.I. will maintain an aggressive turnaround time on Superior requirements and Superior support queries.

COMPANY OVERVIEW

D.E.I. Management Group, Inc., founded in 1979 by Stephan Schiffman, has long been recognized as one of the nation's premier sales training companies, delivering skills and management programs for organizations ranging from *Fortune* 500 companies to start-ups.

Using face-to-face training and distance learning programs, we help organizations do what they do better by effecting measurable improvements in the most critical aspects of the sales process:

- Effective prospecting
- Efficient execution of the sales process (Face-to-Face and Telephone)
- Productive management of prospecting and selling activity

To date we have trained more than half a million salespeople in North America, South America, Europe, and Asia at more than 9,000 companies including Aetna, Blue Cross, Blue Shield, Nextel Communications, Boise Office Solutions, Cox Communications, Fleet Bank, and Datamonitor . . . to name a few.

Who we are:
- Twenty-three-year-old international sales training and consulting firm with the "power to transform your career and help you post noticeable increases in your numbers" (Amazon.com)
- *Selling Power Magazine* credits President, Stephan Schiffman, as America's #1 corporate trainer for prospecting and appointment making
- D.E.I. has offices in New York, Chicago, Los Angeles, Toronto, Dallas, and London. D.E.I. has delivered training in North America,

South America, Europe, and Asia in D.E.I. principles to more than 500,000 salespeople/managers at more than 9,000 companies.

RIGHT TO AUDIT

D.E.I. acknowledges that Superior reserves the right to audit documentation, records, books, insurance, and receipts directly relating to the provision of services.

VALIDITY OF BID

D.E.I.'s bid is valid for a minimum period of six months from April 21, 2005.

PROGRAM OVERVIEWS

Phase I: Introductory Sales Course

Appointment Making

Participants will learn to:

- Develop and practice a proven telephone prospecting approach
- Overcome common objections quickly and easily
- Get more return calls
- Set the appointment

Getting to "Closed" (Prospect Management)

Participants will learn to:

- Categorize each and every sales contact within a patented, visually-oriented six-category system
- Strategize forward movement in the sales process
- Master the system through customized Superior learning tools
- Avoid investing time and energy in dead-end leads
- Project income accurately
- Hit income goals

High Efficiency Selling Skills
Participants will learn to:

- Prepare for the meeting
- Control the flow of the conversation
- Accelerate the sales cycle
- Ask the right questions
- Close the sale

Phase I includes: extensive videotaped or Phone Coach role-play sessions, case-study and mock Prospect Management System profile analysis, and group critique of role-plays.

Follow-through programs can be developed to include: E-learning reinforcement tools and live and/or teleconference refresher sessions with D.E.I. trainer.

Phase II: Intermediate Level Sales Course

Advanced Interviewing Skills
Participants will learn to:

- Find out about the target company's competition
- Find out about current key suppliers
- Find out about your contact's business allies
- Understand past, present, and future buying criteria
- Understand the "how" and "why" of current buying patterns
- Learn about the contact's personal and career goals
- Generate referrals and identify other key contacts in the account

Getting to "Closed" (Prospect Management)
Participants will learn to:

- Categorize each and every sales contact within a patented, visually-oriented six-category system
- Strategize forward movement in the sales process
- Master the system through customized Superior learning tools
- Avoid investing time and energy in dead-end leads
- Project income accurately
- Hit income goals

Phase II includes: extensive videotaped role-play sessions, case-study and mock Prospect Management System profile analysis, and group critique of role-plays.

Follow-through program can be developed to include: E-learning reinforcement tools and live and/or teleconference refresher sessions with D.E.I. trainer.

Phase III: Intermediate Level Sales Course

Account Penetration Workshop

Participants will learn to:

- Uncover past buying patterns and future buying criteria
- Understand the effect of all buying influences in a complex sale
- Develop Pre-/Post-sales strategies to anticipate and effectively deal with anticipated issues
- Understand prospect purchase position prior to entry into Superior sales cycle
- Understand the role and strategic importance of the manager in the sales process and identify critical points of involvement
- Understand when, how, and why to involve other key players
- Role-play the next meeting

Getting to "Closed" (Prospect Management)

Participants will learn to:

- Categorize each and every sales contact within a patented, visually-oriented six-category system
- Strategize forward movement in the sales process
- Master the system through customized Superior learning tools
- Avoid investing time and energy in dead-end leads
- Project income accurately
- Hit income goals

Phase III includes: extensive videotaped role-play sessions, case-study and mock Prospect Management System profile analysis, and group critique of role-plays.

Follow-through program can be developed to include: E-learning reinforcement tools and live and/or teleconference refresher sessions with D.E.I. trainer.

Phase IV: Sales Negotiations Course

Negotiation Workshop

Participants will learn to:

- Define negotiating
- Develop a presentation plan
- Defend Superior's value
- Identify critical information about the prospect and his/her organization
- Identify when to delay (and when to walk away)
- Help your negotiating partner look good to his or her internal constituency
- Master the eight fundamental principles of negotiating:

I. The goal of negotiating is to end up with a better deal than could have been achieved without negotiating.

II. An effective daily prospecting routine improves your negotiating position.

III. To negotiate effectively, you must be able to identify the most important interests of each side.

IV. To negotiate effectively, you must be able to develop creative options that allow both sides to broadcast a "win" to their constituents (boss, colleagues, shareholders, etc).

V. To negotiate effectively, you must be able to identify an outcome that both sides will recognize as "fair."

VI. "Knee-jerk" discounting of price is the lowest form of negotiation.

VII. You must never enter a potential negotiating meeting without a backup plan.

VIII. The next best thing to actually negotiating from a position of strength is acting as though you are negotiating from a position of strength.

Phase IV includes: extensive videotaped role-play sessions, case-study profile analysis, and group critique of role-plays.

Follow-through program can be developed to include: E-learning reinforcement tools and live and/or teleconference refresher sessions with D.E.I. trainer.

Phase V: Managers' Workshop

Coaching for Increase Productivity Workshop

Participants will learn to:

- Understand and interact effectively with the most common personality types
- Build a successful coaching plan
- Set goals that will motivate and inspire individual salespeople
- Learn one's strengths and weaknesses as a coach (through online self-discovery exercise)
- Structure the coaching meeting
- Conduct effective one-on-one coaching meetings
- Build a long-term coaching plan for the team
- Revise the plan to reflect changes in the market, changes in departmental goals, and changes in staff

Phase V includes: online self-assessment exercise, pre-work evaluation of members of the sales team, extensive videotaped role-play sessions, case-study analysis, and group critique of role-plays.

Follow-through programs can be developed to include: E-learning reinforcement tools and live and/or teleconference refresher sessions with D.E.I. trainer.

Phase VI: Executive Selling and Strategy

Major Accounts Workshop

Participants will learn to:

- Develop and refine a Major Account Mapping Worksheet
- Identify key and secondary contacts
- Detail and critique your activity within the account to date
- Identify key constituencies within the target organization
- Identify a growth/action plan for account penetration
- Review the plan with the D.E.I. trainer and with the group
- Finalize an action plan that expands your network within the account

Phase VI includes: pre-work evaluation of major account history, Major Account Mapping Worksheet exercise/discussion, extensive videotaped role-play sessions, case-study analysis, and group critique of role-plays.

Follow-through program can be developed to include: E-learning reinforcement tools and live and/or teleconference refresher sessions with D.E.I. trainer.

TRAINER BIOGRAPHIES

D.E.I.'s team of professional sales trainers delivers the highest quality programs in the training industry. They have experience across a wide variety of companies and industries and with every type of sales force. Your D.E.I. trainer's job is to work with you both before and after the program to ensure that we meet all training goals, that the program matches precisely with what your organization does, and that you are satisfied with all phases of the training process.

Steve Borromeo

Steve brings a wealth of management, sales training, and sales experience to the organization. He joined the company in 1987. Steve has had the opportunity to teach, coach, observe, and mentor 30,000 sales professionals, ranging from financially successful veterans to the most junior new hires. With a background as a competitive swim coach, professional entertainer, salesperson, and sales coach who learned to be successful using D.E.I.'s techniques, Steve injects humor, passion, and a strong dose of reality into each presentation. He has delivered motivational speeches and workshops at international events, and regional sales meetings for large and small audiences worldwide, for clients such as Blue Cross/Blue Shield, AT&T, GE Information, Motorola, ExxonMobil, Lexis/Nexis, Merrill Lynch, Chase Manhattan Bank, Cohen Financial, EMC, and others representing virtually every commercial and industrial category.

Andrew Norad

Mr. Norad brings more than 40 years of sales, training, and sales management experience to D.E.I. Management Group. He is a former High Altitude Survival Instructor for the United States Air Force, and was also a principal at Techniques, a consulting firm instructing job seekers and human resource professionals in interviewing techniques. He is D.E.I.'s primary "train the trainer" specialist, and he is also responsible for training D.E.I.'s new sales hires. Mr. Norad has delivered D.E.I.'s programs to salespeople from more than twenty different countries, and has delivered programs throughout the United States and in South America, Canada, and Europe. He has experience in virtually all industries, as well as in the government and nonprofit sectors. Mr. Norad has been with D.E.I. since 1997, delivering programs for a variety of major clients including: Blue Cross/Blue Shield, Sprint, AT&T, Nextel Communications, Fleet Bank, Siemens, Sun Microsystems, and Prudential.

Ten Things Every Salesperson Should Know

Salespeople count things all day long. They count the number of appointments they have every day. They count how many calls they make and how many of those calls result in appointments and sales. They've even been known to count their money before the sale closes.

In short, salespeople love numbers. Here, then, is another number that can help you close more sales: ten things every salesperson should know.

1. **Have ten stories about how you have helped ten clients.** Knowing the facts about how you have helped your clients is essential information during a sales call. Fancy proposals and outlines are nice, but future clients want to know why they should do business with you. Give them the tangible, quantifiable results—the hard numbers.

2. **Know why your No. 1 account bought from you and how the sale took place.**
In addition to hard numbers, business professionals like stories. Make sure you know why your largest account (the account that now generates X thousand dollars a year) decided to buy from you. The story will break the ice and give you credibility.

3. **Know your top five references and have them ready.**
People don't like to take chances in business. Have ready a list of references your client can contact. Make certain your references are solid and will speak highly of your organization. If your references are respected within the industry, the endorsement can carry a lot of weight.

4. **Know five restaurants in which to discuss business.**
You should always know five restaurants to which you can take a client anytime. Requirements should include good food, service, and rapport, and an atmosphere appropriate for conducting business.

5. **Understand your clients' business.**
Know your clients' numbers, not just your own. Ask how many years they have been operating, how many employees they have, what their budgets are for your services. Understanding your clients' business leads to more sales for you—it's that simple.

6. **Know your top ten target prospects.**
It is common for a prospect to ask you what other businesses you are targeting. The prospect wants to know (for instance) whether you're experienced and well equipped to work with a company of his or her size and industry focus. Asking who else you're reaching out to is a good way for your prospect to discover your firm's direction and capabilities. You should be prepared to offer a list of relevant target organizations.

7. **Identify three internal people you can call on for assistance on a sales call.**
Don't be hesitant about asking someone who has had more experience than you do to accompany you on a sales call. Getting someone to come along on your next meeting may mean the difference between striking out and hitting a home run. A sale still counts, even if you have help making it!

8. **Know your ratios.**
Salespeople often downplay the importance of ratios. Understanding your ratios means improving your sales. For example, if you know that every twenty-five cold calls leads to five appointments and that five appointments lead to one sale, you can work backward to determine exactly how many cold calls you must make to reach a certain number of sales each week. Just do the math.

9. **Prepare for the objections you'll hear.**

If you've been selling for more than a month, you can probably anticipate the negative responses you will hear from your prospect. Will
the prospect say you're too expensive? That your company is too inex-
perienced? That you don't have the right team in place? Prepare relevant success stories: stories about satisfied customers who got more
value than they expected, or who benefited from a new outlook, or
who sang your team's praises. Practice these stories—they will help
you turn the most common objections around.

10. **Have one good joke that always makes you laugh.**

Sometimes business can get stressful. Always have one thought,
story, or joke "in reserve" that can put a smile on your face and help
you keep things in perspective.

About the Author

Stephan Schiffman is president of D.E.I. Management Group, Inc., one of the largest sales training companies in the U.S. He is the author of a number of bestselling books, including *Cold Calling Techniques (That Really Work!)*, *Power Sales Presentations*, *The 25 Most Common Sales Mistakes*, *The 25 Habits of Highly Successful Salespeople*, *Asking Questions*, *Winning Sales*, *Make It Happen Before Lunch*, *25 Sales Skills They Don't Teach at Business School*, and *Stephan Schiffman's Telesales*. Schiffman's articles have appeared in *The Wall Street Journal*, *The New York Times*, and *INC. Magazine*. He has also appeared as a guest on CNBC's *Minding Your Business*, *How to Succeed in Business*, and *Smart Money*. For more information about Schiffman and D.E.I. Management, please call (800) 224-2140, e-mail *contactus@dei-sales.com*, or visit *www.dei-sales.com*.

Index

Other Titles Available From Stephan Schiffman, America's #1 Corporate Sales Trainer

Trade Paperback
$10.95 ($15.95 CAN)
ISBN: 1-59337-155-1

Trade Paperback
$9.95 ($15.95 CAN)
ISBN: 1-58062-857-5

Trade Paperback
$9.95 ($15.95 CAN)
ISBN: 1-58062-856-7

Trade Paperback
$10.95 ($17.95 CAN)
ISBN: 1-58062-813-3

Titles Available in the Successful *25 Sales Skills* Series

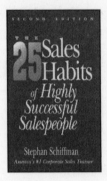

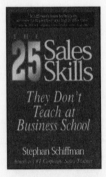